Reading Everyday BODY Language

Become a Human Lie Detector

BY **SANJAY BURMAN**

Published by BurmanBooks Inc.
260 Queens Quay West
Suite 1102
Toronto, Ontario
Canada M5J 2N3

Cover design: Tracey Ogus
Interior design: Tracey Ogus
Editing: Anna Watson
Proofreaders: Olivia Pacanowska
TU Dawood

Distribution:
TruMedia Group LLC
575 Prospect Street, Suite 301
Lakewood, NJ 08701

ISBN 978-1-927005-31-6

Printed and bound in The United States of America

Dedication

I never set out to learn the science of body language. It started to happen when I was treating people who had gone through serious trauma in their lives and would not speak. I eventually was able to pick up on certain universal signs, became curious and that led to studying more about it. So, I would have to thank all my hypnosis teachers, Debbie Papadakis, Harvey Simon and Don Mottin.

My parents who put up with a lot from their strange son.

My editor, Anna Watson, project manager and right hand, John Manikaros, designer Tracey Ogus who made an incredible cover as well, and proof-readers Olivia Pacanowska and Tara Dawood. As well Bruce Rosenberg who has been there from the start..actually before the start! Phil Kent, Bob Baskin and Matt Soble who have the same patience level as a kindergarten teacher when dealing with me! One day I'll get them to snap!

Chantal, who showed if your passion is sincere and you eliminate the judgment of others, a champion will be born.

Introduction

To get the most from this book, follow the rules.

1. Eliminate your ego.
2. Be observant. You have two ears and one mouth for a reason. Shut up and listen.
3. The biggest mistake you can make is thinking you know yourself. You don't.
4. Do the exercises since they will help you fine-tune your skills.
5. With great power comes great responsibility... or something like that. Just sounds deep.

On to the good stuff.

Table of Contents

Chapter 1

LOOK AT WHAT I SAY!

Reading people has two equally significant requirements. The first is seeing others while the second is truly seeing yourself. In using the techniques I describe in this book, you'll gain insight into both sides of that coin so you can avoid unnecessary mistakes and deal with people more effectively in your personal and professional life.

There was a girl I was crazy about. On her birthday, I set up an entire day of fun. I had her meet me in the morning and took her north of the city to The Sugar Bush to sample fresh maple syrup. Then we went to a spa where she got a massage, and then back to my place where I had prepared dinner. Because she had recently graduated from university, I bought her a watch and to throw her off, put it in a cigar box. When I gave her the box, she burst out into tears... not tears of joy, but sadness! She looked at me and explained that the last person she had smoked a cigar with was her ex-boyfriend. She realized she still had feelings for him! It was like stepping in cow shit with no water hose in sight. In fact, getting her to even open the box proved to be a task. When she did, I might as well have thrown the watch out the window since all the attention was still on the cigar box. I didn't have the heart to tell her I had the watch engraved with a message telling her I loved her.

Not having access to a time machine, I was able to turn the situation around by being able to read her reactions and know the words that would most empower her to move out of that emotional state. By the end of the evening, she was cradled in my lap and her snot was on my shirt. It just doesn't get better than that!

And yes, I'm more romantic than the cover would lead you to believe.

This book will give you the tools to accomplish similar feats based on truly seeing your own behavior as well as that of the other people around you – if, and only if, you can follow these three rules:

1 **Eliminate your ego.** Try to take your own feelings out of the equation and act dispassionately.

2. **Be observant.** You have two ears and one mouth for a reason. Shut up and listen and really take in what is being said both verbally and non-verbally.

3 The biggest mistake you can make is thinking you already know yourself. You don't. **Set aside your preconceptions** and be open to the truth.

See and Hear

I'm hoping that by the end of the book, you will see what you are not being shown and hear what is not being said. Just because someone laughs, it does not mean they are really happy. How do they dress? Where do they look when greeting you, directly in the eye or somewhere else? How would you describe their handshake? What is their body telling you? These are just some of the ways that people broadcast their true thoughts - no matter what they actually say.

Eyes

They truly are the windows to the soul.

The following guidelines are given from the perspective of you looking at the person. So where it mentions direction, 'left' is your left and so on.

- **Upper right** indicates Visual Memory. When you ask someone about a memory, in order to describe what it looked like, the person will look up and right.

- **Upper left** indicates Visual Construction. If you ask someone to imagine a pink giraffe skateboarding, they will look to the upper left.

- **Direct left** indicates Auditory Construction. For instance, if you ask someone to imagine hearing the sound of a rabbit singing "My Way" in their head, they will look left.

- **Direct right** indicates Auditory Memory. Think of that last great concert you went to - you're looking right. Enough said.

- **Down left** denotes feelings or an aesthetic reaction. This would happen while recalling a smell, taste or feeling from the past. Taste and smell are very closely connected to emotions.

- **Down right** denotes Internal Auditory - it's the direction you look in when you're talking to yourself.

Use Cautiously. Some people have twitches or weak eye muscles which may cause what looks like a negative or positive eye movement, but these are really just their natural traits. Or, if you are dealing with someone like me who is ambidextrous, then I'm using both my left and right hand which affects the direction in which I access my brain.

Culture is another element that can affect body language and eye movement calculations. In certain cultures, it is considered bad manners to look someone directly in the eye and in others, you are to look someone straight in the eyes at all times.

When trying to gauge eye movements and what they mean, I go more by feeling and less by logic. When someone looks at me in a certain way, I might get a bit of a shiver and want nothing to do with them. I was approaching a very well-known author and speaker about the possibility of coming to our company. He told me thirty times about the fact that he likes win/win situations. At one point, he looked at me from the ground up and then back down. I got such a cold feeling from him that I ended the meeting. I later found out that he was not an honest guy.

Remember: Very dark, big retinas indicate bottled anger - or they are on mushrooms!

You will see reactions in split second glimpses. When you see someone's eyebrows rise, it shows surprise or confirmation. So if you accuse someone of something they did and at the point you accuse them, their eyebrows rise, it shows they are aware of the truth. It can also occur at a point of accusation, in that case showing that the person is surprised and holding back.

EXERCISE

Find a partner for this. Since you show unwanted signs through your eyes, you have to condition yourself to project the right signs. So without using any facial muscles and therefore not making any facial movements, try to have the other person guess what emotion you are portraying through your eyes only. Try projecting strong and diverse emotions like happiness, sadness and anger. Remember, your face should look the same through all of them since you can't use ANY facial muscles whatsoever.

Keep practicing this until any emotion you want to exude can be guessed by anyone. This is an enormously powerful tool you can use anytime you want to persuade or negotiate. Great intimidators who say little but possess the ability to inject fear into anyone have mastered this persuasive art.

Sizing someone up

Pictures never lie. The camera sees what it sees, good or bad, and there are some things that even Photoshop can't erase.

The people who never show their teeth when smiling are fascinating because they usually love being in pictures, but they are always hiding something. Sometimes it's braces or unhealthy teeth but sometimes it's something as significant as their motives.

Then there are those people who don't even really smile. They use their facial muscles to move the sides of their lips up, but it's not a smile. A real smile produces wrinkles or crow's feet on the outer sides of the eyes along with creases around the mouth. Look at press pictures of me. I hate the whole process of doing a shoot so much and I have to make a real effort to smile. So while I might get my lips to smile, if you look at my eyes, you will not see wrinkles on the sides of them; instead, you will see an uncomfortable glance. Another great example of this phenomenon that you can check out anytime would be stars as they walk down the red carpet. Most of them would rather eat my mother's brussel sprouts than be photographed in an uncomfortable surrounding like caged animals - and you can see it in their eyes no matter how much wattage they put into the smile. (If you didn't get it, my mother's brussel sprouts are not good.)

People who are not genuinely happy smile the same way in every picture. In fact if you put all their pictures together and flip through them quickly, the background and people around them change but their faces never do! It's quite interesting actually. Your face is what represents your own life in your consciousness. You can't help it. When people smile the same way in every picture in a rehearsed way, their faces represent their lives to themselves - boring and uninspiring. Most of my high school pictures are like that. If you go through Facebook pictures, you will see great examples of this. Look for those who are in pictures with a lot of people all the time - never on their own or just with one or two other people. Party people are usually depressed individuals who don't like to be alone often. Their smiles will be the same in all pictures.

Profile pictures are particularly insightful. Some of us profile only our face, which could mean that we aren't happy with the state of our bodies, and some profile only the 'best' features, as in a photograph taken from a very specific angle. Some guys flex their abs and some women will show major cleavage and only part of their faces. Drawing attention to the body or a body part is a way of deflecting attention, - ironically, to compensate for the qualities they feel they lack.

People who fixate on their bodies are not only insecure, they are often extremists. I dated a girl who was a personal trainer and she made me nuts about working out. She had to have only healthy foods and follow a healthy lifestyle, which for her included yoga. The repressed side of her was depressed. Sometimes she would cry for an hour, but instead of dealing with the issue that was causing her pain, she would go for a run.

Most people who are extraordinarily fit are making up for perceived inferiorities. I was coaching a female body builder because she was not achieving her best results and her body was almost giving up. We realized that her bodybuilding was a way of mentally defending herself from her ex-husband who had been physically abusive. She was training so hard and taking steroids not for a mere competition, but rather out of a sense of self-preservation. This was about overcompensating, like she had to keep bulking herself up to fight him off - except he'd actually been out of her life for some time.

I had another client who was obese. She was very good at her job, very successful and very well paid. She came to me to deal with emotional issues in her personal life. When she regressed through hypnosis, I found out that she had been raped by an uncle and a boyfriend. The weight gain was an attempt to protect herself by rendering herself unattractive to men. She was building a literal wall between her and any male attention. When we addressed the real issue, she lost 60 pounds in two months without even dieting.

Sometimes, the obvious answer isn't the right one though, and you need to dig a little deeper. Look at me for example. If you look at my pictures, most of them were taken at social functions standing next to beautiful women. The probable conclusion would be that I was not great with the ladies when I was younger, lacked self-confidence and now I am trying to make up for it by showing off how many pretty ladies I know. In actual fact, many women approach me because of what I have worked to become and that makes me incredibly insecure and careful around them. I'm always looking for their ulterior motives. Therefore, if anyone was trying to sell to me, using beautiful women would be the wrong angle. If you were going to sell me, the best way to go about it would be:

a) to show how I can excel (I'm in the self help world, so there must be something in me I'm searching for answers about) or

b) offer something reliable (the idea of being able to count on someone or something gives peace to a person trying to achieve).

Don't be too hasty to draw conclusions solely on pictures. Pictures never lie, however, nor do they offer the whole truth. Even if the person doesn't have an obvious issue they are covering up, it's there so if you spend some time talking to the person to get a bigger picture, you will get at the truth.

Before attempting to read someone, it's essential to meet them in person. Here are some ideas on what to look out for:

1. A person's choice of adornments and accessories often reveals their insecurities.

How much makeup is a woman wearing? The more she wears, in general, the more insecure she is about her looks. Get around her insecurities by complimenting her on something that is God given, for instance her eyes or her hair.

Cigars are big, bold and expensive. Thus, cigar smokers want to be recognized. They are often insecure about the past and have faced poverty. Compliment them on their talent, experience or their wisdom.

The bigger the briefcase, the more detailed the individual. The smaller the briefcase, the more direct the individual. The former never forgets. The latter is more likely to be temperamental.

If someone peers over their glasses to talk to you, they are trying to intimidate you. A person who takes their glasses off to listen or while the room is silent is thinking. The one who wears sunglasses indoors is insecure and has something to hide. Look at poker players. This of course doesn't apply to those who just had surgery on their eyes.

It's interesting when you watch someone answer questions that are making them uncomfortable. For instance, I was out for lunch with a high school friend of mine. He was insisting that I go to his young son's birthday party which involved go-karting and a barbeque. I agreed and then asked if the boy's mother was also invited. The body language that I observed was very interesting because it displayed an uncomfortable reaction to my simple question.

My friend took the drink menu from the table and started to play with it subtly. He looked down at it when he answered and looked up at me only after he finished the thought, but not the answer. "Naw, she doesn't need to be there, she can have her own party for him." Then he looked up, "I invited her for the first one after we broke up, but now it's been 6 years," he added.

The great part was at that moment, the waitress interrupted us. She had served us before and she thought the fact that I order a grilled cheese sandwich at a 'corned beef deli' was hilarious. Every time she came out to talk to us, when I'd ask her a question, she would look at me and answer...while covering her wedding ring. This would happen every single time. Now, I'm not a GQ Model, but my life changed when I removed the hump from my back and came down from the clock tower!

Let's analyze their reactions. My friend who played with the menu and looked down is actually saying that the animosity between him and his ex-wife hasn't been resolved, but there is shame there because he feels sharing a child and having an amicable relationship would probably be easier on the kids and himself. His ego prevents him from going any further.

The waitress on the other hand flirts subconsciously and likes the 'feeling of being single'. She isn't going to cheat...just yet anyway. Her marriage has probably hit a dry spell, but not necessarily because of them, just life. Intrigued, I asked her what her husband does. Turns out he is a music engineer teacher but used to be a waiter up the street. My follow-up question was to ask how often she worked. Her response was 6 days a week. So that being what it is, how much fun do they get to have together? What are they going to do when she has been running around on her feet all day? The relationship is going to take a hit.

2. Pets tell all.

I have a friend who is 33, single and working two jobs to make just barely enough to live. She is overweight and does whatever she can to avoid relationships. She doesn't like herself or her life. She may deny it but her actions prove otherwise. The kicker is that she has a huge Rottweiler that takes a lot of money to feed. The dog is very smart. The dog knows if she growls or whines, my friend will give her attention.

When my friend and I were watching a movie on the couch, she asked me to move so the dog could sit on her. No kidding! The dog was chewing on a bone while sitting on her. I was busy watching them, so I couldn't even tell you what movie we were watching. The dog dropped the bone and my friend picked it up. The dog dropped it again and she picked it up again. This went on 28 times (yes, I counted). That's when I realized, she is the pet; the dog is the master.

This occurs when you shut down your ability to connect to another human being for fear of being hurt. You transfer that emotion to an animal who won't leave you. There is a man who lives in my building and every time I see him on the elevator, I dread it. His dog could pretty much take a shit on my shoe and he would say in the most effeminate voice "Poochy, come here. Please? Come on Poochy buddy." Even the dog looks at him, wondering when he will realize that it will never work! We all know people like this. They have lost the desire to connect with human beings and have made the animal human.

A pet's death is devastating to these personality types. I had another friend who kept her dog's dead body lying in the kitchen all day. The body had actually started to get rigor mortis when I got there. She wanted to keep it another night and stuff it. I had to use hypnosis on her subtly for her to hear any reason. She finally had someone collect the dog's body and she and I went out to dinner to get her out of the environment. I also thought that I might run into a well and hear someone say, 'It puts the lotion on the skin', like I'm in *Silence of the Lambs*!

These types of personalities are very loyal and fall very hard in love. They will treat you well, but because of their past history in relationships, you don't want to use or intentionally hurt them because they will use all their past pain towards going after you. They are also very needy and will want you around a lot, which is something they get from animals.

Another great way to measure the household is to observe the dog. If it is very angry or hyper or even disrespectful to the owner, there is chaos in the household. If the dog is submissive and almost sad, there is an abusive environment in the house, whether emotional or physical. An ideal household would be where the dog is happy, playful, respectful and gentle.

3. Lisps.

I have found that people with lisps often suffer from bouts of immaturity. They will initially come off as confident, put together and focused, but after a very short while of knowing them, their 12 year old subconscious seems to come to life, such as still living a frat lifestyle or being in junior high level relationships. The lisp seems to be a method of freezing a lost moment in time. Some of my friends have lisps and at work they are exceptional while their personal lives are warm. But while some elements of their lives seem commendable, some part of it always seems to be at an early teen stage.

4. Obesity.

As a hypnotist, you are taught that there is an emotional explanation for everything that happens in the body. Yes, genetics plays a role, but it's the trigger we are interested in. You may be more susceptible to a drug addiction than I am, but the addiction itself (drugs, alcohol, gambling) is the symptom of the problem. It's the same with obesity.

The three factors for weight gain are:

- ***Culture:*** A person's culture may be very restrictive and ultra conservative, so a person would gain weight to keep themselves from breaking cultural rules.

- ***Family:*** Family values can cause depression, anxiety and anger should they go against your personal value system. In rebelling without losing the family bond, weight gain is a visual rebuttal.

- ***Sex:*** If a woman or man has been sexually assaulted at an early age, they might express their pain through weight gain as a way of making themselves less attractive to the opposite sex. A client I was treating lost most of her extra weight when we discovered she was raped twice before the age of 14.

BEFORE you get upset, no, I'm not saying because you are overweight you are trying to be unattractive. You may be extremely beautiful. So before you react, read the other two rationalizations and see which one belongs to you. Yes, one of them does. Even in my own case being overweight, I was sexually assaulted in the change room showers of a gym my family belonged to when I was in Grade 2. I didn't think it had any effect on me, but I had so many body issues growing up and still do that I know my weight problem can be traced back to the fear of it happening again.

Behavioral Clues

You project your thoughts and intentions even when you're not aware of it. Here's how to recognize patterns of behavior that you can observe in other people.

- Watch for excess energy

Excess energy gets dissipated into fidgeting, a definite sign that someone is nervous or ill at ease. These people will unleash on you in a second's notice if you trigger them. Bouncing legs, tapping with fingers, clicking of pens, chewing on gum and constantly looking around all are signs.

Janine Driver, aka the "Lyin Tamer," body language contributor to NBC's Today Show and CEO of the Body Language Institute suggests you never touch your face, throat, mouth or ears during an interview.

The interviewer may think that you're holding something back - typically, the truth. Although this may very well be a false assumption, avoiding the act of touching your face or facial area is very good advice when you're trying to establish credibility.

I was the judge in a talent contest for the East Indian community. It was on a national broadcast and the creator of the show said to us that in the final round, he was getting the biggest Bollywood star to appear. Within a second of completing that statement, he scratched the back of his neck. I knew that he had not solidified the deal.

- Hands and arms

Clasped hands are a signal that the person is closed off to you. A palm out gesture at shoulder height is a sign of openness and calmness. Hands or arms over the shoulder signify a desire to keep control over others, like Hitler and the Nazis. People who want to show they mean no harm will put their palms out and pump their arms slightly at the person who feels threatened. Some people who try to calm a crowd will put their hands over their heads, palm down, giving the adult to child control gesture. If you observe this kind of situation, you'll notice the person will not be able to calm the crowd easily. We don't like the idea of being controlled.

To come across as confident, receptive and unguarded, have your hands open and relaxed on the table. When your body is open, you project trustworthiness.

Avoid crossing your arms over your chest. It shows that you are either close-minded, arrogant, defensive, or bored and disinterested.

When you see someone rubbing their palms together slowly, run fast! It is a devious gesture. Look for it when people are explaining a deal to you. When you see fast rubbing of the palms, it is excitement and a positive feeling - for them, not necessarily for you.

- Finger gestures

Yes, even your fingers say something. When you 'steeple' your fingers, as in finger tips touching looking like a church, it shows confidence and arrogance. There is a pinnacle that you are showing the other person that you sit on.

When someone has their hands clenched palm to palm and fingers in fingers, it is usually a sign of irritation or anxiousness. Politicians who are at a podium being asked questions from the press will sometimes go to that pose if asked a series of questions they don't want to answer.

- Hands behind the back

Some people walk around with their hands behind their backs or holding their wrists. This is a sign of superiority and confidence. The idea is 'nothing can harm me even when I'm not protecting myself' and you'll often see it in leaders, royalty or certain celebrities who are trying to look modest when touring a place or walking with another leader.

Sometimes, in order to see the message a person is projecting, you really have to observe the whole body and how the small actions combine. As I was putting this all together, I was sitting at a coffee shop waiting for someone who had been delayed. I started to watch a woman get two cups of iced green tea and sit out on the patio. This means obviously that she is waiting for someone. She started to scroll and then text on her Blackberry. Being bored, she was in a relaxed position with one foot on the leg of the table and leaning back in the chair with her legs slightly apart.

A few minutes later a tall man with his son and dog came over to the coffee shop. She and the man obviously knew each other and most likely had seen each other around. She got up to walk over and talk to him. The dog jumped on her and she patted him. The son was given some money from his dad and went in to buy a drink.

She made sure her arms were pulled together in front of her, forearm to forearm and she crossed her feet in front of her. She was making herself as small as she could. She would look down and tilt her head at an angle to look up at him with her eyes, showing her neck. He, being a big guy, adopted a stance with one foot spread slightly in front of the other and made large gestures with his arms while telling a story. He was making himself bigger.

Remember, I couldn't hear a word that was being said and was only watching through the window. What I knew for sure was the person she was meeting up with was in trouble, because she had more of an interest in the man she was flirting with.

The boy came back with his drink and watched his father and the girl talking. He started to play with the dog between the two of them. He felt threatened by this woman taking up his dad's time and attention so he started to separate them. The father took the hint and the girl went back to her table. I thought to myself that maybe I was wrong and there was nothing going on. Just as he passed her, he had his phone out and after a line exchanged between them, he started to key in her number. Bingo!

About 3 minutes after he left, the boyfriend came, kissed her and sat down. She went back to her original position with a foot on the table leg, in a leaned back position and arms hanging over the sides of the chair. He sat legs crossed at the ankles, under the chair, arms on the table leaning in and more into what she was saying than the other way around. She is the boss of that relationship. This is a woman whose beauty has probably gotten men to feel insecure and assume a whipped role in order to keep her - which actually bores her. She longs for a big man to take control and be protective.

EXERCISE

Shut the sound off on your television and watch politicians, preachers and journalists as they speak to their audience. It is amazing to see how clearly their bodies are rejecting the very things they are saying.

Now that you can hear their bodies, try it again while you listen to their voices. Does it match your assumptions?

The Motivations Behind the Behavior

You'll truly understand how to read someone when you understand the kinds of motivations that lie underneath the behavior you're observing.

One of the most common motivations is overcompensation i.e. going overboard to give one impression when what lies at the heart of it is something entirely different. You can watch for the signs of overcompensation. It applies to so many aspects in life.

In some ways overcompensation is to show how genuine the emotion is. For instance, Italians are notorious for using big hand and arm gestures when talking passionately and East Indians are notorious for shaking their heads side to side slightly when in agreement with their own words or your own. But sometimes overcompensation is about compensating for other things, like insecurities. For instance when you see someone who is constantly fixing themselves or looking in the mirror, that person is insecure about their looks – even if they are extremely good looking. They might not have always looked that way.

Insincerity can also be the root of overdone or overcompensating behavior. If someone is going on and on about how much you have to get together soon and how great you are, it's a sign there is there is overcompensation to mask opposite feelings.

Let's look at the girl who dresses provocatively and how about the guy who gloats about how many women he has seduced. All of these people are overcompensating for their insecurity which is actually the opposite of what they are trying to prove they are. For instance, the girl who dresses provocatively might actually be attractive and the guy might have really slept with a lot of women - but not to the point that they believe it's true. Their actions will tell you a different story, revealing their hidden insecurities about being unattractive or that guy who never gets the girl. Even when they - to an outside observer - seem to have achieved some degree of success in those areas, the deep seated insecurity still drives them to push farther and farther to the point of excess and overkill. They can never feel sure about it and obsess about how others see them.

As I keep reminding you, actions speak louder than words. What you can see from someone's actions is their state of mind. For instance, let's say someone finds out they have a winning lottery ticket for $5. If the person states, "Big deal, now I'm rich" sarcastically, they are probably not in a good place emotionally and most likely feel they get the bad end of the stick most times and this is just one more example of that. However, if the person says, "Wow, maybe I should go to Vegas since I'm hot right now", they are quite positive and generally happy people. Even the small things please them and lead them to have more positive thoughts.

You walk into a room. Your friend is sitting at the computer and is typing away. You say, "Want to grab a pizza?" and your friend flies off the hook with, "God, you just threw me off my thought process! Now I have to start all over again. And no, I don't want pizza, I'm always forced into having pizza. Just go and I will catch up. Leave me alone." Your eyes have not even blinked and the shock has not left your body. As you leave, you are wondering how you could have been so thoughtless as to ask your friend to join you for a pizza while in the midst of the most important email of their life! In fact, this email could have changed the course of history and now mankind is doomed forever!

Wrong. This has little to nothing to do with you. A great technique to confront someone and at the same time find out what is wrong is to start with 'Is it possible..?' For example 'Is it possible you are upset over something that has you so irked you are not even able to identify it?' Or 'I'm sorry for interrupting, but is it possible you are angry at something other than the harmless pizza?' The minute you take the passive approach and start with 'Is it possible', you are not stating a fact, but asking them to think about it from an observational perspective thereby letting go of the emotional hold for even just a second, but long enough to calm down. Normally, the person is pretty embarrassed for yelling at you like that even though they might not say it. Great time to ask for money though!

Evaluating a person's mental and physical reaction is a great way to judge their level of self-respect. A person with a lower sense of self-respect will act entirely based on ego. If you make a joke at their expense, they will overreact. If you win at a game, they will keep playing until they win and will take any loss - even at a game between friends - very personally. These are people who can't let go of any slight or perceived disrespect. Self-respect is about how much you like yourself and how you see yourself. A healthy sense of self-respect gives you a buffer against these everyday occurrences. But for someone with low self-esteem, being right and coming in first is the most important thing and they'll pursue it at any cost.

A person with a high level of self-respect may be beaten at a game and admit to defeat...this time. They will want to learn how to not lose again. If you make a joke at their expense, they will laugh it off or come back with a joke themselves in a tasteful and non-aggressive way. They really have no need to prove anything to anyone and are comfortable in their own skin. They have confidence and so they're not driven to overcompensate.

Communication and Perception

These two elements also lie at the heart of what you can learn about how people act and react. People reveal themselves in how they communicate and even in the words that they use.

When I give lectures on hypnosis, I often say that we talk 'at' people more than we talk 'to' people. Ideally, you want to have the other person do all the talking. Human nature makes it so we love to talk about ourselves. The best interviewers on television listen more than they talk. They will let the person they are interviewing tell them what the next question should be. If you give them a chance, people will reveal their personality and also, how they process information.

We process information one of three ways: audibly, visually or aesthetically.

You can tell how someone processes information by the choice of words and expressions. For instance, if they use 'I felt' or 'I was shocked' or 'I was hurt', they are aesthetic thinkers. The best move you can make is to show effort and thoughtfulness in the details. For example, if it's someone you're dating, have a candlelight dinner. Cook the dinner yourself and if possible give the mood a very romantic feel with soft music.

If someone typically employs expressions like 'I saw' or 'I wore' or 'It looked like' more often, they are visually inclined. Visual thinkers love expensive gifts. They will also notice details, so don't wear the same shirt two days in a row! Audible thinkers will often say 'I heard' or 'She sounded like' or 'All you could hear was...' A perfect gift for audible thinkers would be a unique CD, tickets to a concert or an orchestral performance.

EXERCISE

Consider the following examples and attempt to categorize them correctly:

- Example 1: A woman complains about a date's blabbering. She describes how turned off she was, even how she raised the volume on the stereo to quiet his incessant talking.

- Example 2: A baker who describes the difference between French bread and

Italian bread by the cut on the top and how the cut changes the look, but not the taste or texture.

- Example 3: A woman describes being with her husband on a Sunday evening watching movies, cuddled in his arms on the sofa, relaxed and stress-free before the new week begins.

Hopefully you correctly identified the first person as someone who processes information audibly. Her comments all revolve around sound - and yes, this type of person can't tolerate big talkers. The second person is a visual thinker. His conversation deals with visual aspects of the bread and that's how he evaluates it. The third person reacts aesthetically. This woman's conversation involves feelings and emotional associations.

If you can learn how to evaluate a person's choice of words along these lines, they are basically giving you a manual to their processing methods. Start talking to people in general, whether you know them or not, and see how quickly you can detect how their brain processes things and which methodology would best be used to communicate with them.

Remember we ALL have three processing avenues (unless you are blind or deaf), so just because someone happens to say, 'I heard', doesn't necessarily make them audible. If you can't figure it out, revert to aesthetic. We all feel. This is why when I'm giving a lecture to a large crowd, I always use aesthetic words and phrases to communicate to the majority.

JOURNAL EXCERCISE

Talk to ten people. Mark down the gestures you see them make in regards to the conversation. Also make note of the type of words they use and evaluate them as being aesthetic, audible or visual. Once you get in the habit of doing this, it will become easier and easier to pick up on the clues that will allow you to get a handle on how to best communicate with them.

Chapter 2

MY HYPOCRISY HAS ITS LIMITS

REALLY??

My Chaos Theory

Always keep the chaos theory in mind. Simply put, it's this: behind what is clearly expressed often lies an incongruent truth.

Put into practical terms, if you can read people, you can understand why they do the things that you hate. Upon understanding this, they will no longer upset you since you will understand the motivation behind their actions. Either that or you will know how to attack their insecurities until they crawl into a fetal position and weep to the sounds of Kumbaya. Just kidding... well, not entirely.

"What you repress, another will express," Dr. John Demartini (a human behavior expert and founder of the Demartini Institute) said so eloquently. It means that for every emotion that you hold back, someone else will express it. Any habit, emotion or action that is brought about by someone who irritates you is merely a reflection of a repressed mirror inside of you. Change what you repress and watch how the dynamic between you and the other person changes. The action, emotion or habit will either dissipate or that person will stop coming around you as often. Most importantly, what aggravated you before will no longer aggravate you in the future.

I was with a banker who was in charge of an investment division. His clothing was pristine, hair perfectly set and he sported a tan that looked natural.

After analyzing him, I discovered he was insecure in his job and his image was his mask. Either that, or Fabio was his idol. Sure enough, his daughter had assumed his suppressed qualities by not achieving her potential; she was afraid of her image. He talked about the fact that she was a good athlete but that she was not achieving her full potential, intimating that she was too afraid of what other people thought to take her abilities to the next level. Seen through my analysis, rather than addressing his own issues, he focused on hers.

Also consider the incredibly clean person married to the incredibly dirty person or the overachiever married to the underachiever. You wonder how that happened? I see my ex with her present husband and I have to read this book aloud just to make sense of it! It is not as simple as the attraction of opposites. Each partner is suppressing the opposing aspect of the other person's personality. The only way they can express it is by getting involved with somebody who contains that quality. Human dynamics are just that simple.

The question is how do we change that? Are we stuck with a mate who is unorganized and filthy? The answer is no. The way to change that quality in the person is to change whatever quality you don't like in them, in yourself.

If you've been cheated on or abused, think about how you may have done the same to someone else. Let's take a woman who always gets into abusive relationships. The first question is: who did she abuse to get into the vicious cycle? As harsh as it sounds, the law stays the same. Could it be that she has been accepting of those relationships because she has been abusing herself? Or, could it be that she tolerates abuse from a boyfriend or spouse but expresses herself in an abusive manner to her best friend?

The thing about the chaos theory is, it can also work for you. The famous saying, 'You have to spend money to make money' doesn't only work in an economic sense, but also in a natural sense according to the laws of the universe. The basic law of physics is whatever goes up must come down and that every action has a like reaction.

I had a problem with an assistant to someone I was working with. You should always be very good to those who work as assistants to executives. They can get you in the door. This assistant was giving me a hard time and preventing me from reaching my goals. My lawyer and I were having lunch and he said,"Just go to the executive and tell him what is going on behind his back!" I thought about the chaos theory and I realized it would only cause problems. So, instead, on my trip to India, I bought her a silk scarf. It didn't cost much there but the return on the investment was 400%. She became my best friend and biggest ally. She was also fired three weeks later. Maybe the moral of the lesson is to smother the person with kindness no matter how harsh they have been and they will either quit or get fired. It's not quite that simple, but they will quit getting in your way.

There are no victims in the game of reading people, there are only players, and there are no loopholes either. The Chaos Theory applies to everything and everyone. This is why learning the rules is so important. No gesture, look, word or action is done by mistake. It may not be happening consciously, but the brain's subconscious is 10 times more powerful than our conscious brain.

As I was writing this book, someone I had just ended a relationship with a few weeks earlier called my cell phone. As I went to answer it and saw her name on the phone (you know who you are!) she had just hung up. Well, I laughed because she may say she did it by mistake and she may be right...consciously. Subconsciously she may have been thinking about me for some time or had an experience that reminded her of something I said and her finger 'accidentally' called.

I was teaching a hypnosis class and showing people in the class how easy it is to read them by doing it in less than 60 seconds when one of the students asked if I might be reading too much into my analyses. I turned to her and told her that she is someone who probably suppresses bad events or thoughts and tries to deflect conflict in the hopes that it will fix itself. She was taken aback but ultimately, she confirmed my claim.

The universe's law is always black or white. By trying to facilitate a grey, you're only cheating and victimizing yourself while losing the opportunity to gain. A grey attempt would only be your ego trying to achieve a fictional superior stance that doesn't exist. You achieve an authentic superior stance when you can read and understand others, identify strengths and weaknesses in yourself.

You know it's a lie when...

The human body is a natural lie detector. The only people this does not apply to are psychopaths or sociopaths. Other than that, our bodies react to our thoughts. Some of the signs will occur in 1/8th of a second, but they are still present. The subconscious and conscious are constantly battling. The subconscious is a child who is very open and does or says things independent of what our conscious mind wants to communicate. Tell someone a lie. Make a conscious effort NOT to give away any signs. You will still feel the smallest sign force itself out of you like swallowing hard, a twitch, or in even more extreme situations, sweating. Even though your conscious mind will verbalize whatever lie you want to tell, your subconscious will act out the guilt.

The first things to look for in spotting a lie are contradictions. For instance, a person who lies may not avoid eye contact with you. They may stare you straight in the face. The difference between a stare of interest and a stare of confrontation lies in the pupils. If the pupils are constricted, the person is getting confrontational. They will shift their body away from you ever so slightly and they will scratch their ear, nose, neck or head. They may even frown when they make a statement. 'It's good to see you' may be followed by a very quick smirk. No, this is not just an itch or a regular facial movement, these are tell-tale signs.

Specific Lie Indicators

You'll see one such indicator when the hand covers the mouth even slightly. It might only be one finger, but what it signifies is the body rejecting the words that are coming out. Here are some others to look out for:

- **Extending blinking**. The person will blink longer than a normal blink or they will be blinking rapidly. Look at interview shows on TV. Whether it's a politician under the spotlight or a movie star talking about their latest film, some of their answers come with enough blinking to cause a workout sweat!

- When you see the **'Shh' gestures** being used by an adult to another adult, it's indicating something that shouldn't have come out of their mouths. This is a subconscious gesture that reflects back to childhood when parents gave you that sign to keep quiet.

- **A split second touching of the nose**. I was being interviewed by a radio DJ who kept asking about one of my books. She said that she was very busy and therefore had no time for a relationship. I told her as she scratched her nose that she had experienced a very bad break up and kept herself busy to avoid getting attached again. She stuttered and moved to another question, laughing nervously.

- **The neck;** touch on the back of the neck or the side indicates discomfort with their thought or statement.

- **The eye rub** indicates not wanting to see the truth, or embarrassment.

- **The ear tug** is validation of a satisfactory lie to themselves.

- **The collar pull** signifies discomfort from telling a lie. In my book, *Do Everything They Tell You Not To Do*, I describe Shoshanna Lonstein, the girl of my dreams, modeling her lingerie designs by placing them in front of her and asking me what I thought of them. I go on to write about how I responded with a simple, "Nice", and then tried to unbutton my collar, which led to me pulling my button right off. Obviously, I thought it was more than just 'nice' and she laughed.

Regardless of the object used, such as fingers, cigarettes or pens, touching the lips or mouth is an attempt to feel more secure. Contact with the lips recalls the comfort of breastfeeding.

Delayed reactions are clear indicators of a lie. For instance, I love watching people open gifts. They will say they love it and stare at it for about a second before finally following with a smile. Sometimes I give a bad gift just to see if the person is honest. If you give them something they don't really like, notice the smile without wrinkles, see that stare at the gift and then see how they thank you. It will be with a hug that involves a pat on your back or a handshake that is quick and then a stare back at the gift. If you add in 'Now don't you go and give it to someone else!' you'll see the eyebrows rise and the uncomfortable laugh that follows, showing discomfort and realization that their body had already planned on doing just that.

Pay attention to the objects which are placed between you and the other person. They may have a book, toy or even pen that they will fidget with. This is a way of subconsciously putting space between you and them in order to protect themselves. I remember confronting a woman about her drug addiction in a restaurant. She was so embarrassed that she looked down and smiled subtly. She had the drink menu standing up and was fidgeting with it like she was semi-reading it.

Warning: Don't come to quick conclusions until you have studied the person for at least a minute to see if they have a natural twitch, dry skin or back injury that deviates from normal circumstances.

EXERCISE

You can do this out loud or internally. Look at yourself in the mirror. See yourself at least up to your waist. Now with belief, tell yourself a lie. State your name is 'Bob' for all that matters (unless your name is really Bob). Stare for 3 seconds.

Now, you did something as you said it, even if it was said internally. What was it? Some of you swallowed, some of you twitched and some of you scratched your neck or cheek. Some of you had a completely different tell-tale sign.

Even when you know you are going to say a lie, your subconscious will still reject it.

Negotiations

When you are involved in business or any other type of negotiations, it helps to know where you stand - and the signs go well beyond (and may in fact contradict) the other party's words.

Here are some of the signs to watch out for:

- Head tilted up slightly and chin forward is a sign of defiance or superiority. This person wants you to know they are bigger and more powerful than you.

- If the legs of the person are on a 45 degree angle with the body, it means they are not really comfortable with you and their legs want to walk out the door.

- If they have crossed their ankles, usually under the chair, they are getting irritated or anxious.

- If a man crosses his leg over his lap, he is presenting a free-spirited but powerful image. However, a woman will not do this even if she is projecting the same image since it will send a sexual signal. A woman will generally cross one leg over the other. This is a demure, sophisticated and intelligent look.

- A subtle head movement from side to side before you finish your sentence means the person is rejecting your idea.

When someone removes their glasses to clean them unnecessarily or cleans dirt off the pants unnecessarily it is a sign the person is rejecting your idea and trying to distract themselves from having to hear any more of it. I was in a pitch meeting at the studio and as I told the executive about the script concept, he kept flicking a piece of lint off his shirt. I stopped talking about the script and started to ask him about his son who was pictured on his desk starting baseball. Needless to say the movie wasn't made.

Leaning back, sometimes with a foot on a table or chair and a slight laziness in their speech pattern is a sign the other person is disinterested and unengaged.

If you feel that your speech, interview or introduction is not going well and you are seeing negative results in the other party's body language, you can change it simply by making physical adjustments.

For instance, move a few feet to the other side, make a sudden arm gesture when you come to a strong point or be quiet before strongly delivering your key point with a little rise in your volume. You should get back their attention.

If you want to find out if there is any interest in an idea or proposal, leave the question open ended. Curiosity will only arise if a person is interested. Let's say you don't want to come off as eager or desperate but you want to find out if there is any interest in a professional scenario. You could make a generic statement like, 'I'm looking for a great designer, if you know of anyone that would be interested in working with us, please let me know.' Based on the response, you will quickly be able to gauge their level of interest. If the person replies with 'I will keep my eye open', there isn't much of a response but if they reply with numerous questions about details like pay, timing, and so on, then you know there is a lot of interest from their side.

More TIPS for Negotiations

A common mistake for people is to think that in a negotiation, one wins and the other loses. The best negotiators get what they want and make sure the other person gets close to what they want so no one goes away mad. Should the time come for the two parties to negotiate something else in the future, there will be no hard feelings. However, in a negotiation, wouldn't it be great if you could read the other person's mind? You can. Here is a summary of what you should keep in mind when in a negotiation of any kind.

1. Listen to the person. Ask them what they are looking for and let them talk. In fact if they talk for 20 minutes straight, let them. Most of it will be white noise and you may want to fall asleep, but just when you least expect it, a piece of vital information will come out of their mouths. Like we have discussed earlier, people love to talk about themselves and you have two ears and one mouth for a reason, so listen more than you talk and you will find out everything you need to know.

   I had a person talk to me about how there was 'no way' I was going to get a deal out of them for their book. "I don't need you,"' he said. Without taking it personally, I just asked him a few questions and eventually about his past.

Without even thinking about it, he started to tell me about his past deals and how he was taken advantage of. Perfect, now I know where the resentment comes from.

2. During the conversation, recite back to them what you've just heard. This makes it clear you are listening and also there is no chance for miscommunication – even to yourself. Sometimes if someone makes a comment that is hurtful to us, we hear it differently than what was really said. 'Sometimes what you say is boring' can be taken as 'You are boring', however that is not what was said. When you repeat it, you clear it up for yourself and they know you consider them important.

I always recite back to people what they said. Don't do this as an imitation of the person or as a mockery of them or it will create anger. I know this personally! And I hate the fact I have to write this, but without getting into detail, trust me when I tell you that it's a situation you don't want to be part of.

3.   Let them know of your goal and make sure you insert their words in the sentence. This makes it clear to them what the end result is going to be.

Up until now I've talked about how to observe and react when it's the other person doing the talking. When you do the talking, phrase your conversation from a perspective of feelings or aesthetically as I've discussed earlier. This is a language common to all human beings because we all can feel. Some can't visualize as much as they can hear, but all of us have aesthetic processing as our second most prominent way of understanding if not the first. So, when I respond, it would sound like this: "What I am going to do is figure a way for us to receive the loan while putting up collateral that makes you comfortable." See that I use the affirmative. We ARE going to get this done, so relax, and on top of that, you will be comfortable. Soothing, comforting and strong all at the same time. You should see the other person's body language relax when I slip into this mode of communication. If you are truly sincere about what you say to people, if you look at their eyes, you will see a slightly wide-eyed look not to the point of fear, but of interest.

4. You have heard what they have stated are their concerns, what they want and why. You might have a bit of a backstory of their past history. Now that you are armed, frame a deal that gives you what you want and incorporate what they want. This is where a bit of push and pull will take place. They will want 60% of what they want, and you will want 60% of what you want. The more you get closer to meeting at 50% you will see their body language change from crossed arms or furrowed brow when they hear something they don't like to a slight smile or leaning in more when they do.

Use their body language to gauge when you are on the right track. You can practice by watching people in a restaurant or at a coffee shop. Watch them without being able to hear what is being said. You will be able to see when something resonates positively or rubs them the wrong way with something negative.

CASE STUDY

Read the following scenario, which dealt with a situation that you might call 'extreme' negotiating. At the end, make an evaluation as to what I should do. The scene is a true story and I was involved.

It was a very hot summer's day. Driving on the highway, the cars were forced to exit by the police. Being that all the cars on the highway were now using the city streets, there was a traffic jam. Adding to the heat, the situation was really frustrating.

As the cars eased forward slowly, we came across a park with hundreds of people staring across the street and pointing cameras. As I looked in the same direction, I saw a man standing over the bridge railing, threatening to jump off the bridge onto the highway below. There were police everywhere and two cops were yelling back and forth.

The suicide threat was a scruffy man in his late 20s and his khaki coloured bomber pants were slightly stained in the front - probably from holding the rail of the bridge. His t-shirt sported the logo of a motorcycle company. He was screaming with his chin cocked forward but his body was leaning back over the 40-foot drop.

The police had surrounded him in a semi-circle, but were keeping a safe distance from him. A couple of them had their hands on their sides, not quite on their guns. The wannabe jumper then started to shout orders while flailing his right arm around.

I had two choices:

> A. I could use my experience to create a rapport and talk him down.

> B. Or, I could go home.

Read through the case again to figure out what I should / did do.

ANSWER:

It was too hot and I wanted to get home to my air conditioning.

The reason I could leave the scene comfortably was because:

- Chin cocked shows arrogance as he looked down on the police (like I do when I get speeding tickets).

- Yelling at the cops shows room for negotiation.

- Arms flailing in front of a large crowd shows he is seeking attention - not looking for a quiet way to end his suffering.

Because he is interacting with the crowd, the police and enjoying the attention, there is room for negotiation. He obviously shows contempt for the cops so he has most likely been in trouble before and is showing off his superiority over them.

Finally, he picked a spot with a 40-foot drop. He may fall, but only to break a bone or two - not to die. If he was serious about his threat, he wouldn't want a lot of attention and he would be experiencing shame. He would pick a higher place to jump from to guarantee death and he wouldn't have time to talk; he would be focused on jumping.

I went home.

How Body Language can work for you...or against you!

I happened to be reading about famous chess player, Bobby Fischer. It started after I saw a great little movie called *Searching for Bobby Fischer* and learned about how chess players can become mentally unbalanced later in life if they get too absorbed into the game. The constant paranoia of the game and the strategy of trying to figure out what the other person is going to do can overtake your mind completely to the point you lose all perspective in life. This happened to Mr. Fischer.

However, before that happened, he was best known as being the top chess player in the U.S. at just 15 years of age. His most famous game, and probably the most famous chess game in history, was Fischer against the reigning World Chess Champion, Boris Spassky. It took place in Iceland in 1972 and the match took the headlines away from Watergate and all other world news stories. This was good versus evil, democracy versus communism. It was going to determine which country possessed the most intellect. Literally, people made this chess game that significant!

Fischer knew that and also knew too much was on the line. He made the paranoia work for him. First, he started by complaining about the fact that it was being held in Iceland. It was too small and too far away. Then he started to complain about the fact the winner's pot was too small. The Icelandic, American and Chess Organization teams worked around the clock to appease him. They found an additional sponsor and doubled the pot to $250,000, along with granting him a percentage of potential television and film rights. They waited...and they waited. Fischer went to JFK airport and as soon as the paparazzi took a picture of him, he turned, ran out of the airport, got into a car and left. I know you didn't read anything past 'paparazzi', right? Yes, they had those even in '72.

Everyone was thinking Fischer was already crazy and unstable. However, he was just getting started. Then National Security Advisor (and future Secretary of State) Henry Kissinger called Fischer and asked him to get on the plane because the U.S. really needed this game to happen, most likely because they wanted to take media attention off the Watergate scandal.

Fischer finally got on the plane to Iceland, where Spassky had been waiting for 6 days now. Muhammad Ali did something similar when he went up against George Foreman for the famous 'Rumble in the Jungle' of 1974 that took place in Zaire (now the Democratic Republic of Congo). Knowing Foreman was stronger, Ali had to beat Foreman with mind games and confusion. Ali didn't really allow people to see him training. What he did show the public was him walking the streets, talking to Africans, going to the concerts – almost taking the fight lightly. This throws off your opponent.

Finally, July 12, the day of the chess match arrived and Spassky, the officials and the viewing audience around the world waited for Fischer to show up... and waited. With only minutes left on Fischer's clock, he arrived, shook hands with Spassky and made his first move. Relief flooded the nervous and stressed out Spassky.

He made an error many found surprising in the first game, one that a player at his level shouldn't make. Fischer ended up resigning the game, in effect giving the win to Spassky after 56 moves when it became clear he couldn't win.

After more complaints about the cameras, he delayed the start of the second game and then demanded that the clock be reset. When it wasn't, he refused to play and the game was forfeited to Spassky.

At this point, Spassky had won the first two games and Fischer didn't come off as the chess prodigy that he was. And yet... observers noted how unnerved Spassky was becoming with Fischer's erratic behavior. The officials, the viewers and most importantly, Spassky were losing it! Can't we just play??

Chess masters being interviewed all over the world said the match was over since Spassky was 2.5 points ahead and coming back from that is near impossible at that level. Fischer I'm sure was aware of that... or at least knew that would be the perception. Most people expected Fischer to forfeit the tournament and leave Iceland; many believe a second phone call from Kissinger tipped the scales in favor of Fischer staying.

But, just like Ali did in taking the first punch from Foreman and saying to Foreman in his ear, 'Is that all you got?' Fischer was throwing his opponent off by presenting a scenario beyond what he was used to encountering. Fischer had felt Spassky's first punch and essentially took it lightly.

They moved the third game to a small, closed room that had no spectators and was outfitted with a single mounted camera shooting footage of the most celebrated chess match in history. The move, a concession by Spassky, turned out to be his undoing. Once he arrived at the backstage room for the match, Fischer stopped to inspect the television equipment. Boris, already seated, was visibly agitated as Fischer took his time. Fischer began with a simple move that he'd rarely even used before, throwing off Boris, who'd studied his moves. Fischer went on to win the match - the first he'd ever won over the Russian grandmaster.

Game 4 was returned to the auditorium but Spassky's nerves were so on edge from the whole ordeal; Fischer almost not showing, then complaining, then not coming on time, then having cameras removed, then losing the first and second rounds, and now he'd lost to such a simple move. He was not able to think properly. The situation was not helped by his own team telling him that Fischer was just playing with his mind! As Spassky began to lose game after game, the Russian delegation began to make their own demands. At one point, they accused Fischer of using a concealed device to mess up Spassky's brainwaves. The match was stopped and police searched the entire auditorium. Now Spassky was even more thrown off by looking like an insane individual.

Fischer continued to play completely differently than he ever had before, keeping the Russian guessing. At one point, Spassky was defeated so badly, that even he got up to applaud Fischer. By September 1, Spassky withdrew from the tournament and Fischer took the World Chess Champion title.

If we evaluate it, Fischer didn't spend time talking about how he would beat Spassky; he never even recognized Spassky in any of his complaints or erratic behavior. Never once were they directed at his opponent. If you were to point behind someone at something on the wall, the person would look behind them. If they see nothing, they will look at you like there is something wrong with you. If you do it again, they will look again and then back at you like you are crazy. If you do it yet again without pointing, but just staring, they will start to get paranoid thinking there might be something on the wall that they are not seeing. If you did it another time, they will start to check often because you have put doubt in their minds. Never once did you say 'look' or 'what's that' or even 'I'm going to make you paranoid'. All you had to do was subtly instill the doubt and let them do the rest. This is a great tool to use, especially if you are trying to gain an advantage.

Most people do this when they are outmatched. Ali and Fischer knew that the odds of losing were much higher than winning if they went head to head. So, the best move was to throw their opponents off by simple actions that would weigh heavily in the minds of their opponents and be distracting enough to swing the scales to their advantage.

IT'S NOT A LIE, I LIKE YOU

You know they are into you when...This is fun. It is amazing how we men get lazy once we have found our woman. It's true that women will also often relax their standards once they're firmly inside a steady relationship. But, up until that point where you become truly comfortable, *are they into me?* is a question that's often on your mind, no matter what your gender.

When meeting someone new, you need to focus on the body language and micro-gestures that you'll be able to observe. This short list summarizes the signs that will give you insight into what the other person is really thinking.

1. A man likes to be the hero or protector. Therefore we instantly make ourselves 'bigger'. Look at the peacock. He will spread his feathers to show the female how big, powerful and good looking he is. So, a man will bring his shoulders up and out, he will either put his hands in his pocket to add width to his frame, or he will put his arms in a position that will make him look bigger than he is.

2. A woman will do the opposite because she wants to seem dainty and so she will make herself smaller by bringing her arms together in front of her body, or bringing her arms closer to her body at least. Her legs will be closer together, in some cases, she will actually put one leg behind the other.

3. If he sits, generally, he will sit with his legs further apart; again, it's about taking up more room, showing how much of an alpha male he is.

4. She will cross one leg over the other, or sit with her knees together.

5. She will naturally start to 'pretty herself up' by playing with her hair, licking her lips or in some cases, very very subtly purse her

lips. It's all subliminal on her part. If he starts to purse his lips, well, if it turns you on, more power to you!

6. He will be leaning in to talk to you. He's interested in everything you have to say, yes, even about the latest shoe sale.

7. He will be taking you all in...visually. A man is less subtle, so he will be looking at all of you and you might notice him looking at the parts he is most attracted to. It could be your hair, eyes, mouth and yes, chest - but that's a sign that the interest is more sexual than romantic. If he's constantly staring at your chest, he's looking for sex. A man interested in romance would (also) be noticing the more subtle features and your face in particular.

8. Look for sincere smiles on both parties. Crinkles around the mouth and outside of the eyes.

9. Their breathing will line up with yours if you establish rapport. If you don't know what rapport is or how to establish it, you need to read the rest of this book!

10. A woman will retain eye contact with a man she is interested in. If she is constantly looking around and does not appear very

interested in what you are saying, she isn't into you...or you have been married over 10 years.

A man instinctively needs to be the bigger one and in control. We are the protectors and we do things unconsciously to prove that.

For instance:

- A man will stretch and let out a groan almost as a sign of power and strength. Lions, apes and birds do the same thing.

- He may put his hands on his belt, or his hand may rest near his crotch or on his upper thigh. These are signs of ...well, it's not hard to figure out what he's thinking about.

- Men usually sit with their legs apart. This isn't just because we are lazy and it feels comfortable, it's also being romantic in an ape-man sort of way.

- A man will stand close to the woman and may put her against a wall to show protection and a sense of 'guarding' over her. Women play up to that instinctively.

Women have their own set of values to live up to in the game of connecting with the opposite sex. A woman usually does the following:

- Will play with her hair to show she is very feminine and wants him to see how pretty she is (unless she has lice).

- She will make herself smaller. Women buy the smallest shoe they can fit on their feet, the clothing that most accentuates their most feminine physical traits and will stand with her arms tucked into her body slightly to show a demure, soft image. When a couple is getting romantic, he will bring her into his chest, and she will tuck her arms into her chest while he holds her. These are the dominant/submissive roles being played out.

- A woman will also expose or bring attention to her neck and lean into the table to show undivided interest. You might actually see their heads tip to the side slightly just to fully expose their necks. This also gives you the side of the neck they are most sensitive on, so if you get to a romantic stage, you can stroke that favourite side of her neck very gently with your fingertips. Again, a romantic stage, not the running into someone at the grocery store stage. Not cool.

Finally, they're into you when...

- The eyes widen slightly and the eyebrows go up, even if it's only by a millimetre. I was not subtle as a teenager, so I would literally stare into a girl's eyes to see if her pupils would dilate when she was talking to me. If someone is excited or stimulated, their eyes dilate up to 3 times their original size.

- If she looks up slightly and her eyes have to go up to see yours, it is a submissive and fragile sign and she is looking for protection from you.

- The slight pouting of the lips, almost like a kiss.

Some signs are typical in both men and women. If you see these, the other person is definitely interested.

- If the person is hesitating leaving a room, inching closer to leaving, but slightly looking back to see where you are and if you are following.

- A true smile is on display when laugh lines are displayed around the cheeks and eyes. This one is a little difficult with the invention of Botox, but for those who still remain pure, any smile that does not produce laugh lines is not a genuine smile.

Once You're Dating

Once you've both admitted to the attraction and you begin dating, there's a whole new set of body language that will help you know what's really going on between the two of you - or that couple you're observing.

A couple's hitting it off when they start to mirror each other. For instance, if he puts his head on his hand while leaning on the table, she does the same. If he laughs, she will as well. There will be 'accidental' or 'joking' touching going on. If he says something funny she may laugh and give him a bit of a push or hit on his arm playfully. While walking, their hands may touch once or twice. She may even rub her chest against his arm.

If you hug someone and they pat your back in return, they are not comfortable with the hug and want out.

'We' to 'She' is a very telling sign in conversation. You go to dinner with another couple. He tells you about last night, using the term 'we' when narrating. "We went to dinner and then to a movie. As we bought popcorn, she ran into an ex-boyfriend and then after the movie, I took her home." Uh-oh. From the collective we as a couple or team, he deflects to she, separating himself from her. There was no Barry White played that night!

On a personal note, if you know someone likes you, you can get them to campaign for your attention. By stating something like 'I'm looking for someone who likes movies, dinners and dancing', you will get a reply that is a way of selling you on them. 'I like movies too, what kind do you like?'

Sometimes, you may be getting all the right signals and a relationship based on real attraction seems like it's in the works. You begin to date and then... somehow it just doesn't work out. What seems so promising fizzles out and you never truly know why. Did you get the signs and body language wrong? It can go deeper than that; you may have been dealing with someone who's conditioned themselves to sabotage relationships.

• **The Bitter Committer**

If you have been unsuccessful at love with someone you have had a true connection with, it may be that you or they are a Bitter Committer. This is a person, usually very attractive, who jumps from one person to another without getting into a real relationship. They may start by seeming very interested but before long, they act cold and uninterested in any sort of long term possibilities and seem to break up with ease. When we give all of ourselves to this kind of person, we think they are evil for being able to move on with a blink of an eye.

Well, here is the truth about our cold-blooded evil lovers. They are actually in more pain than you can ever imagine. They have come from abusive relationships, whether physical or emotional. They have been so badly hurt that they have hardened themselves to never go through the process again. However, late at night, when your head is on your pillow, you are unable to lie to yourself. These people truly want to have a loving relationship with you, especially if you open yourself up to them completely. The fear of pain simply overrides their feelings for you and they will leave.

A common excuse for their behaviour is, 'I'm just looking to have fun' or 'I am not a commitment type of person.' Or the best one is, 'I don't see anything wrong with having a lot of sex.' This is funniest when it comes from a woman. They replace emotional fulfillment with physical fulfillment and then make themselves believe that it's the sex they crave when in fact it's the emotional satiation they yearn for.

The closer you get to them, the sooner they will run. They'll repeat the pattern until they are ready to risk the pain in favour of deep fulfillment. If they never get to that point, they often get involved in convenient marriages. This is where they never truly give themselves to the other person, but live out a married lifestyle in order to fit into our cultural system. In a lot of cases the marriage will end or infidelity occurs, or both. Either way, without the risk of pain, they will never fully appreciate themselves or their partners and this is one situation where the only healthy thing you can do is leave before you get too emotionally attached. You will never get true intimacy from them until they are willing to do what it takes to change.

• The Litter Committer

You may also encounter the exact opposite personality. This is the person that will commit to anyone at any point! They litter their lives with commitments to people they haven't spent a lot of time with; they'll commit at the drop of a hat. They are so full of fear at being alone that they would rather be in unhealthy relationships than healthy ones. They rarely leave and never cheat. They have to be broken up with and cling like rubber cement paste. They feel they lacked love and try to make up for it by wanting to be loved by anyone and everyone who will have them no matter how unsuitable or even abusive.

The good part is they are very loyal to you if you get involved with them. Bad news is that they are like the in-laws that never leave.

In some cases, past experiences leave severe and long lasting scars on a person and will affect their close relationships for the rest of their lives.

• Survivors of Assault and the after effects

People who have been molested, assaulted, abused or raped are usually emotionally scarred. They feel towards certain people the way you would feel if you were involved in a terrible car accident at a particular intersection. You would be very careful when driving near that intersection after that and would probably try to avoid it all together because you'd shy away from the memory of all that pain. We all have a mechanism for avoiding pain that plays itself out in different ways; the more severe the source of the pain, generally the more severe the reaction.

When we discuss these people who have experienced something tragic like sexual assault, the signs are very important to read. Depending on the person's value system, the age that it happened and the specific situation that took place, it will be acted out differently. However, the survivor will ALWAYS act it out. Their bodies are in pain, fear and anger, all of which it can express themselves in different ways.

A girl I went to high school with was considered if not the prettiest, then certainly one of the prettiest in school. All the boys wanted to be with her and from the outside she looked like she probably had the greatest life ever! She confessed the truth to me years later when she told how the other girls had hated her and due to jealousy, tortured her emotionally and sometimes physically. She went on to tell me that her parents had a strict curfew so she wasn't able to go out at night like most high school kids do and the boys all just wanted to sleep with her, which made her paranoid about men. The after effects of this shocking situation have developed her into a person that can go from 0-100 on the temper scale with only a one word trigger! She can get irate if you question her about just about any topic or if she feels pressured in any way. This is all due to the fact she has suppressed all the hostility from her past and it comes out as a girl with a huge temper. It really doesn't matter if the original incident happened in high school, at home or in a relationship, anyone with a hair trigger temper is really lashing out at a specific incident and anything or anyone that can remind them of the past. We usually pass it off as someone who is difficult to work with or whisper 'Bitch' under our breaths, but really this is a person in pain who is trying their best to run away from it.

You have to imagine what the person has gone through and then pick your words to avoid confrontation. For example, there is a person I know who courageously survived cancer twice. She is a model, so on top of having her hair fall out during treatment, she was not able to work. One day I said to her, "Life is too short and we should live it up." I didn't say it to her directly, just out loud and in general. She got very upset at me and asked me what I had meant by that. She went on to tell me that I had no idea what I was talking about and that I should stop judging her! Literally I couldn't even put the slice of pizza in my mouth. I was just frozen from her reaction towards a general statement. When she left and I had time to review the conversation in my head, I realized she was lashing out more at herself and the idea that she has confronted death twice and therefore knows more than anyone how short life is. Human error, but one I can avoid next time.

Here are some scenarios where prior trauma could be acting itself out:

•   **Lesbians, Clubbers and Condoms**

I have some friends that are gay and I find it interesting to analyze my interactions with them. In my research of gay relationships I have come to the conclusion that 83% of gay men are truly born gay and surprisingly only 37% of gay women are truly born gay (from the body language and verbiage when asked questions and daily lifestyle habits). One research study, according to The International Lesbian Information Service, states that 50% of women have had lesbian experiences and feelings! When I say 'born gay', I'm referring to people who are only attracted to the same sex and have never been interested in or attracted to the opposite sex. I said this to a gay friend of mine and he laughed so hard because apparently this is an ongoing joke in the male gay community.

Why then are there so many women stating they are lesbians when they aren't? In my opinion these statistics are a result of emotional trauma. They truly believe they are attracted to women but the reason they are is different than the women actually born as lesbians. I had dinner with a friend of mine who is a lesbian for over 15 years now and I get the impression from our conversations that she needs to prove to me that she is in fact gay. The funny part is that she always shows me her girlie side, as in she likes me to drive her car to the restaurant or if she pays for dinner, she will give me the money to look like I'm paying. If you saw us walking together on the street, you would say she was attracted to me (or so my friends and parents seemed to think).

When we had dinner together, she and I got into a heated discussion as I challenged her on her lifestyle. After emotions ran high, she blurted out that her father tried to sleep with her. She went on to say that she had dated men in the past but she didn't feel she was treated well. She then retracted that when I quoted her and she said she was treated extremely well. Sounds confusing? Well now you are getting a glimpse of how confused she is in her mind.

The idea of running to another woman is like nourishment to another woman's soul. She needs to be lightly touched, kissed and caressed with no reservations because she knows she isn't going to have her body ravaged by an imposing or domineering man. In a sense, she is looking for companionship. She feels secure and non-threatened in the relationship.

This friend also feels the need to only go after women who are straight in an attempt to convince them that they haven't yet gotten in touch with their lesbian side. She tried this on my cousin, who came and told me there was no way she was a lesbian. My friend feels the need to express to everyone that she is a lesbian. It's almost like her calling card. Without being one, who is she?

The reason is when her father tried to sleep with her, her identity was taken away. Everyone needs an identity and she gets the most attention out of being a lesbian. Another big clue lies in her choice of women partners. My friend will openly admit she can only go out with other hot girls. She does this to be noticed, and again, it goes to identity.

I have another woman I know who claims to be a lesbian and it's the same story, but in her case it results from a traumatic rape when she was 13. She felt she needed to run from any resemblance to that night by escaping with other women. Both of the women in my examples are not happy. They don't have a steady relationship with anyone and they feel isolated in their worlds, so they work constantly. They are in pain.

Now, there are those women who are naturally attracted only to women, one of whom worked for my parents. She had this very natural male energy about her, even though not all lesbians are like that. But importantly, it wasn't a put on or forced. Scientists have been working for years looking into the reasons for sexual preference, but the answer is not the point of this book.

Don't fall for the girls in clubs who kiss other girls. This is an act of desperation to capture male attention in most cases. If they really are more interested in women and were not doing it for attention purposes, they would go to gay clubs where they would not be bothered or stared at. Those girls carry condoms, and not because they make better balloons!

Gay men are similar. The ones who are born gay know it at an early age. They may date girls in high school to fit in. But a lot of the guys who become gay are emotionally or physically abused by their fathers. They have become so afraid of the alpha male types that they completely rebel and become involved with another man. Why not a gentle woman? Because the abuse has taken them into a shell and they take on a more feminine, nurturing type of personality to give what they were never given.

Remember, not all men who are abused wake up and become gay. This is only with the small percentage that have become over time attracted to males.

• The Slut Phenomenon

'Did you see the girl at that bar last night? Holy cow, she had her boobs pushed almost out of her bikini top and she looked like she was going to make out with that dude at any second!' This is a statement similar to words all young men have stated to each other at one point or another. But the question is, was she really as easy as she looked?

A rule you learn in your late teen years or early 20's is you never go for the hot girl who looks the most provocative; you almost always go for her quiet friend just behind her who is not getting any attention. Of course, I wouldn't know if that's true, since I never did the one night stand thing.

A woman who has been sexually assaulted or abused physically or emotionally will sometimes act out in a constant need of attention from men. She will get their attention by sleeping with them or by dressing provocatively. For us to properly analyze this, we need to go back to the father/daughter relationship. There is a group of women I know who have a healthy respect for themselves. They are in the 28–34 age group and have never slept with more than six people. Many of them told me they believed it was because of their father being so strict with them and wanting to know where they were at all times during their teenage years. One told me that as much as she hated him at the time for always intruding in her life, she looks back and thanks God. Another one told me her father gave her all the latitude it the world and only gave her advice when she asked, but always listened to her. She said that because he never passed judgment, she felt that she had to earn his respect. The important thing their experiences have in common is a father who cared and was engaged with their upbringing in a meaningful way.

When girls grow up with very stern and unemotional fathers who were rarely around, infrequently asked them where they were going or with whom and never really hugged or kissed them, it leaves a big gap in their lives. This caused a need for the girls to get the male attention they were so thirsty for. Even though the male attention they get from sleeping around or flirting with guys is insincere and unhealthy, it's still male attention at the end of the day. They feel attractive, loved and feminine for even just a few minutes. They will look for a dominant male figure and will be extremely accommodating.

A male that has been abused as a child can act out as homophobic, aggressive, angry and in severe cases as a rapist or abuser. Again, they feel so much rage inside for what happened to them, they express it through anger to other people, like they need the other person to feel their pain.

A former trainer of mine has a body of a gladiator, and if he isn't in jail, he's in street fights or training for the UFC. He is yearning to be loved, but is also so trapped by his anger, he has only physical exertion to release his feelings temporarily.

This stemmed from his relationship to his father, who was emotionally abusive to his mother. That was the family life he witnessed growing up - until his father left the family. He had to figure out how to be a man on his own, without a role model, and he developed a lot of hostility because of it. As an adult, he takes it out on his own body - he's full of tattoos all over his bulging muscles. In fact, a lot of people who are very muscular have issues over a fear of weakness. It's overcompensating behavior. Another personal trainer I knew was very badly abused by an older brother as he grew up. He worked out to become huge and muscular out of a sense of self-preservation.

The heiress to a grocery chain is not only beautiful, talented and very classy looking, she is also very approachable. But, if you look into her eyes, they don't change expression even though she might smile or laugh. She is very distant with men and will usually stay in a relationship only for a short time before moving on. Her choice of man is the model look, someone who is in great physical shape. This is important because when you see a very pretty girl with a man who has model looks, it means she has a lot of insecurity in herself and how she is seen in society. She's overcompensating to make absolutely sure she's seen in the best possible light as far as being physically attractive. She is also in lust because love is too painful to experience.

My friend, the heiress, is also into keeping control, so that when the time comes to leave she is not bothered too much by it. She is the type to ask a man to come over for sex, but have him leave immediately afterwards. She has linked sex with a feeling of temporary security and affection. You will never be able to get involved with a person like this if you are interested in the long term until the person wants to deal with their emotional pain and anger towards men. Men can also act this way if they have been hurt by a woman in the past and will act it out by dating only stunning women that they can have control over and thereby show to society how in demand they are.

• Cult Followers

Cults are successful because they give a person what they most need: security, a sense of belonging and love.

A large percentage of people who I have worked with end up getting caught up to a point of obsession in the self help world and even start speaking like they are born from the loins of 'Princess Love'. This new world becomes their universe. They feel they must advertise it, push it on others and spend all of their time immersed in it.

Many of these personalities stem from abusive fathers and these people resort to clubs, societies or religions that can give them emotional nourishment. The positive part is that they really have good intentions. They want the rest of the world to feel as great as they do, but their insecurities also contribute to the fact that they need to feel that they are not alone in this newfound 'enlightenment'.

• S & M

I found out that a person I know went out with a girl I also know, and apparently he likes to have his face slapped and his penis stomped on. It so happens this is what occurs on all my dates, even though I don't like it.

I was treating a single mother who was raped on her birthday by the football quarterback and even though she told me she had resolved those issues, she also loves to be photographed hogtied and whipped. Again, reminding me of my prom night in high school. Getting back to her, she is showing how she feels about herself. There is an element of humiliation and degradation still present in her psyche. Conversely, she also loves to dominate men in bed, which shows anger towards the opposite sex.

Some would judge her as being strange or crazy, but really she is expressing what is inside her subconscious. In fact, I know many adult film stars who retire because they can't take it anymore. They literally feel so denigrated that they throw in the towel hoping to finally rid themselves of that feeling.

Now again, I will state that these are broad strokes and general symptoms. We can do a whole book on each symptom in detail. I just want you to recognize the general signs.

CASE STUDY

All the following women are 28 years old and have been assaulted. Pick which woman has most probably been assaulted before the age of 12 and remember to use not only instinct, but the clues that seem insignificant.

- Girl 1:

Very friendly, very open minded to learning about other cultures and foods. She is like an open book and talks to everyone. She has a close tight pact with a few girls and is well known in the charity and socially conscious world. She comes from an educated background and close family. She carries a small air horn with her at all times and keeps her purse under her arm. She prefers to be accompanied to a garage parking lot rather than enter it by herself and gets a little nervous when walking alone at night and a group of men are behind her. She will speed up to a brisk walk. She dates educated and successful men, but is more turned on by intellectual abilities rather than materialistic trophies. She has a tough father who is very successful and a stay at home mother who is very nurturing.

- Girl 2:

A club girl, meaning she is always at nightclubs dancing and drinking all night long. She has a boring retail job and tells herself she is going to quit, but never does. She will make out with guys and if on a first date, can be convinced to give oral sex. Most of her Facebook pictures show her laughing wildly with her friends and most were taken in nightclubs. She is overtly friendly and always welcomes new people to her social life. She dresses seductively in tight clothing with a lot of skin exposure. She has bouts of emotional highs and lows and when depressed, will cry alone in her room and then go out to party as hard as she can. She sometimes uses drugs at clubs and it's usually ecstasy, but sometimes cocaine. Her parents are very good to her but have little control over her. Her mother is soft spoken as is her father, and they do spend some evenings together every week.

- Girl 3:

Severely overweight. Dresses very provocatively and usually smiles without showing her teeth or crow's feet. She is quiet but can get very loud and physical when provoked. She also goes to nightclubs a lot and loves the attention from guys, but will only go home with the one who plays it cool and distant. She smokes a lot of pot and will sometimes compete with the boys to see who can drink the most alcohol. She likes Ultimate Fighting, Indy cars and motorcycles. She is alone since she has few friends and even the ones she does have are more like close acquaintances. She has a small dog and has little to do with her parents. Her father is a blue collar worker who has shift work and mother is a secretary at a large corporation.

ANSWER:

Girl 3 is the one who has most probably been assaulted by the age of 12. In some cases, the memory has been so far repressed that the survivor has forgotten it and in others, they feel it was so insignificant that it has nothing to do with them in the present. Our Girl uses sex to attract men and is so angry in life that she is unable to show happiness and reacts to the smallest situation. It is easy to tell from her pictures that she is unhappy by the smile she shows in all of them. The way she dresses shows she is trying to attract male attention through the only way she knows how, and her sleeping around and her marijuana use happen to deaden the sadness.

Girl 2 was assaulted, but probably from being drunk or high and ending up in a bad situation. She is always in a group not only because she feels lonely, but also because it will avoid the same situation from repeating itself. Her anger, depression and need for male attention most likely comes from the fact that her father is more of a female role player in the household since he is very soft spoken, doesn't show protectiveness towards her and she feels inside she is not loved by him, even though she thinks that she is logically. A lot of females who come and see me are usually in my chair because they have felt something lacking in their relationship with their father from a young age. The way she dresses seductively without outright trying to look like a prostitute is to get her father's attention, yet keep what little dignity she has left in hopes her father will question her or show some authority as she feels a father should.

Girl 1 was most likely felt up in a public place or may have been the victim of theft at knife point. She is protective of her surroundings and is trying to be less of a target. Due to her strong family support system, she has not let it change her psyche that much however she takes more precautions so as not to allow it to happen again.

Chapter 4

THE PREACHER IS NOT THE TEACHER

Remember that the most religious person at the table will never speak of religion. They understand what God is to them and how he fits into their world and they don't need to sell it to you or anybody else. I know two women who describe themselves as born-again Christians. They spend a lot of their time preaching about other people and what they're doing wrong, but they themselves indulge in one-night stands and have their own drug addictions. However if you talk to either one of them, they will go on, and on, and on about God.

To identify someone's biggest insecurities, just listen to what they preach, whether that favourite topic happens to be religion, happiness, wealth or philosophy. I will go as far as saying that 98% of the time, they live the opposite. You may not see it at first, but if you keep watching the dichotomy will reveal itself. I have a friend that used to brag about how fantastic his life and family were. When you asked how he was, he always said: 'Life is great, life is great!' He was so excited about his answer every time that it would get a little annoying. So, not wanting to but finally giving in to that annoyance, I started to scrutinize his life. It turned out that he was away from his family four days out of seven and unwilling to change that work schedule or circumstances. He went on stubbornly believing it was all working out fine but eventually, the seam ripped and his life was turned upside down when he discovered his wife was having an affair.

Today, when he says he is happy, I believe him because he has come back down to earth and is more conscious of his true emotions and the rose-coloured glasses he chose to wear back then.

Tip: The richest one at the table is the one who doesn't reach for the cheque the minute it comes. The poorest one is the one who reacts immediately. Their actions reveal their concerns right away.

Watch for those who overcompensate for things, like the people who are constantly talking about how much they love their lives or those who need to update you on every tiny bit of good news they receive, but pass it off like it's nothing.

I love 'life coaches' and if you subscribe to my blog, you have seen how I have ripped the term to shreds. Some of the life coaches I have met are failed actresses who simply went on to the next convenient thing! One life coach - and I heard it from a friend that dated her - only eats two cupcakes a day to remain skinny! Yet at the same time, she's advising people on how to live their own lives. A life coach will almost always live the opposite of what they preach. Look for those who admit to their faults and show sincerity towards correcting them. They are more likely to have something to teach you; life lessons come from examining our own actions first. There is also something about integrity. Do you want to be 'coached' by someone who has no integrity and tells you to do something they are not capable of?

I know a woman who is a 'life coach' and who seems to need to tell everyone she comes across details of her professional life like when the TV crew arrives at her house, where she is going to coach her victims - I mean students! Oops. And, she needs to tell everyone how fantastic her life is on an ongoing basis. She never seems to have a bad day!

Wow! I would be envious if I didn't know better. If she is trying to sell me on it, most likely she doesn't believe she is worth enough by just being herself. To compensate, she has to give you this running headline.

A person who is truly happy, truly confident and truly aware of who they are would spend far less time trying to sell you on it. They're just living it. They have no need to emphasize that fact or try to impress it upon everyone they meet.

You can pick up a lot about a person's insecurities in how they relate to others. A wealthy person who came from wealth is less likely to talk about it or show it off as opposed to someone who made themselves wealthy beyond their family background and feels undeserving of their new status. If you drive in a wealthy neighborhood where mansions line the streets, you can see those that need to show off will have the fanciest of cars whereas those who are enjoying their lives and feel less need to show it off will have middle-ranged cars.

So, if you find yourself talking a lot about how happy you are or how well your career is going, or even how secure you are about yourself, ask yourself who you are trying to convince.

I also love those who feel they have to insist on how honest they are. I have met many businessmen who claim to be so honest and have to remind me (more themselves) of that fact over and over. Remember, the rules don't sometimes work on this one, they always work. Remember 'I am not a crook!' by Richard Nixon? That worked out well. What about the politicians who are not only against gay rights, but have to go on the biggest PR campaign to prove it - and then promptly become involved in a gay sex scandal? Or what about when I say I want to lose weight (clearly preaching, clearly)?

Understanding this facet of human behavior means you can use it in your dealings with other people as well as in examining your own behavior and habits.

Reinforcing the other party's obsession is a great technique when you want to know how to make the person feel secure and trust in you. For instance, if you are dealing with an actor who constantly has to tell you how great the director and casting agent thought he was at the last rehearsal or the lawyer who has to go on and on about how they win every case, then you can encourage that sense of trust in you by reciting the key processing words you observe from their conversation back to them. "Wow, you really committed to that character. You are a good actor!" Women do this to the men they are interested in or in love with. They'll talk about something they know is near and dear to their man's heart and reinforce the positive feelings he's looking to validate when he mentions them all the time. It works! The man falls in love with the way the woman makes him feel - great about himself. The woman in this situation becomes the emotional nurturer in this way and we men become reliant on their praises.

A female bodybuilder I know mentions in every line of her bio the fact that she is 45 years old. Now it's great that she is able to keep her physique, but you can see that she is trying to sell herself on the fact that she is 'not' getting older by looking better and better against younger people. She is desperately trying to hear praise for her youthful body. Turns out, she is one of many children and probably didn't get as much attention as some of her siblings so she is emotionally needy now. When she tried to retire from competition, she realized she had devoted all her attention and time to her body and as a result no one knew her outside of the bodybuilding world. When the obsession for attention takes over, it often results in a life that veers out of balance.

When someone preaches but doesn't practice, it's often an unconscious way of making up for something they're afraid of. There are other ways that people can project their feelings and sometimes even hostilities onto you and these aren't always immediately apparent. Here are some elements and behaviors you can spot and ways that you can effectively react to them.

1. When someone is late and keeps you waiting, it is a power play

I'm not talking here about the person who's slightly late occasionally or once in a blue moon. I'm talking about the kind of person who is habitually late and brushes off any complaints about tardiness without a thought even as they overreact when someone else dares to be late.

The message here is clear. They are exercising power over you and showing you how little they think of you. Someone who keeps you late is showing arrogance. They don't consider your schedule or needs important enough to take into account. No matter what your dealings with them, whether it's personal or professional, they will always be more important than you.

When I was in the film business, I came across a real character who was notorious for a lot of things - a big agent in Los Angeles. You could basically say he ran the city. He kept people waiting very deliberately. He would purposely keep younger agents waiting, sitting around outside his office for a half hour or full hour at a time. To his way of thinking, it kept the hierarchy in place and clearly showed them *you're just not as important as me*. No matter what your connection is to the perennially late person, be wary of these people because their needs will always take precedence over yours.

How do you deal with this type of personality? Remember that this is about control and manipulation. The only way to keep your sanity and have some hope of turning it into a productive situation is to keep your cool.

When they (finally) come to greet you, never show you have been waiting. Be busy reading, writing or talking on the phone. Make them wait about 30 seconds until you are done your task. If they are more than twenty minutes late, when they arrive, state very politely that you are late for your next meeting and that you will call them to reschedule. Don't call. They will call you. Don't be upset or resentful, since they will read that and dismiss you. That's part of their game - an emotional response means they got to you, they manipulated you. Also, if they try to set up another appointment, tell them you will get back to them on that and go home to check your schedule. Show that you are at least reciprocating. This is the kind of move that will earn their respect. They may even start paying attention to you!

It's a similar thing with telemarketers. Watch those people who pick up the phone and say, 'Hello?' three times before the telemarketer starts in. The telemarketer can assess the likelihood of having a shot at a sale or completion of a survey based on your patience. If I say, 'Hello?' and I don't hear a response after a second, I hang up. My mother will continue to say 'Hello? Hello?' for the next 45 minutes.

2. Assess the environment

When entering a room, whether it is an office or home, look around. A lawyer I knew used to preach about how money was not important to him. His walls were hung with medieval swords and Japanese warrior furnishings. This showed me that he was not being honest. Sure enough, my bill with him ended up with $322.00 outstanding. In one week, I received two e-mails and one phone call from him requesting the money. Don't be fooled by what people say.

We decorate our personal environments with how we want to be seen. This knowledge comes in handy when it comes to observing and assessing others' behavior because we can detect quite a bit about what they want from life from the environment and the objects they choose to surround themselves with. An example would be walking into a house that is filled with Buddha statues, pictures of Shiva or

Krishna and piles of self help books displayed on the bookshelf, ostensibly all about seeking enlightenment and peace from a chaotic history. This person will most likely bore the shit out of you by preaching Laws of Attraction and so on, but will only practice it themselves when convenient. Most likely they crash the minute something goes wrong and get depressed.

Let's take for example a house displaying books about history, politics, philosophy and poetry. This is a person that really wants to be respected and thought of as intelligent. They know a lot and feel the need to display it thereby showing their biggest insecurity. Somewhere inside, they have a fear of being thought of as stupid or perhaps of not being taken seriously. The best part is that books or bookstore gift certificates are the easiest and best gifts to buy for them!

In a work environment, you can observe how clean or messy a person's desk is. If the desk is messy, the person is scattered and doesn't remember specifics. If the desk is clean, they only remember the broad strokes and will have to review notes and files to see the details. Most lawyers or doctors have clean desks and remember the amount you owe them without checking, but have to check files when you ask, 'Why so high?'

3. The Adrenaline Junkie

We have all seen the adrenaline junkies and some of us wished we could be one of them. I am reminded of the 'mimbo' (man bimbo) Tony from an episode of Seinfeld. Elaine dates this good looking adventurer that George gets a man-crush on. Tony convinces George to go rock climbing and do other ridiculously strenuous things, which George does to look cool in Tony's eyes. I have been there.

I came to study adrenaline junkies when I dated one briefly very recently. She skydived and bungee jumped among all sorts of other crazy activities. These types of personalities are also the ones who will try drugs, party all night and go to school all day. They drive fast, live fast and in some cases, die fast. Why? What drives them?

Simple. They are not happy with their lives and 6 out of the 10 I interviewed had little to no contact with their families. They are depressed to the point that they have to do drastic things in order to feel a sense of euphoria. The very interesting thing that I found was, even though they never admitted it outright, many of them had a death wish. I concluded this when I learned 8 out of 10 of them had attempted or prepared to attempt suicide at a younger age! The idea of the rope possibly breaking, the shoot not opening or falling 200 feet to the ground was part of the thrill since the worst case scenario (death), wasn't threatening. I noticed with the girl I was dating, when I shared with her the small joys that were constant, like how good it felt to be taking a walk beside the lake or just hanging out together for an afternoon - those 'everyday' pleasures - and started to get her to smile and laugh more often, her endorphins would kick in, giving her enough happy feelings that she began to cut out the life threatening adventures.

So when you see an adrenaline junkie, these are physical preachers rather than verbal ones. They will go on and on about how happy they are, how much they love life and yet they prove this by tempting fate, thereby possibly shortening their lives, over and over again.

This does not apply to those who like the occasional rollercoaster ride or will try skydiving with an experienced professional. The above description is for those people who are constantly pushing the limits and can't seem to be able to get positive feelings from life any other way.

4. Crackberry/iPhone Addiction

The addiction to cell phones, Blackberries and other communication devices doesn't stop for these people. They use their devices during movies, social outings with other people and unfortunately, even while driving.

We laugh and make jokes, but it's a true addiction. The addiction isn't with the device itself, it's with escapism from whatever they are doing. I have interviewed six heavy Blackberry addicts and in all six cases, they suffered from bouts of depression. One is very successful at work, pulling in a very large salary, but has no social life and will escape by watching Youtube at a dinner with friends. During two interviews I conducted, both admitted to not having any true friends, so they were constantly typing back and forth to acquaintances in an effort to feel connected to a social circle.

I concluded that this type of personality feels what is happening on the other side of the Blackberry is more important that what is going on in front of them. Messaging also creates a feeling of importance that they normally don't feel and they can't risk losing it by not instantly replying. Spending time with a Blackberry addict is very difficult since their attention span lasts for only a few seconds. However, to combat your companion's addiction, calmly get up to leave without saying a word. This will provoke their fear that they are insignificant and they will respond immediately. They will put the device away... but only until the addiction kicks in again and they succumb to answering all the important people's important questions.

I have a friend who is always on her iPhone - constantly and no matter where she is or what's going on around her. She's completely missing out on what is going on in the present moment. This is a person who often talks about how she wants more adventure, action and experiences in her life but when it comes right down to it, she'd rather talk about her fantasies to her 'friends' online than actually live them. For her, the iPhone is a way of retreating from a reality where she hasn't been able to create any of that adventure and excitement, and instead creates a pseudo-world of virtual friends. The saddest thing is that it's an addiction that's so hard to break. That unreal world is always waiting for her and it seems so much easier to access than anything she might be able to achieve in the real world.

Pay attention to the people who have Blackberries but almost never check it when they are with you. They are much calmer, much more put together, and much more secure with themselves. They also have more depth to their personalities and enjoy life much more.

5. Angry People

Anger comes in all forms.

Uninhibited anger is displayed, of course, when a person snaps and starts yelling or swearing. The easiest way of dealing with this is to bring their energy down to your level, rather than you going up to theirs. Calmly ask: 'Why are you so upset?' The question will prompt a conversation that will divert their minds from what they think they are angry about. From there, push a little more with, 'What are you really angry about? If you tell me, maybe I can help you get what you want.' They will instantly calm down because anger often spawns from simply not being heard. The alternative, yelling something like, 'I can't do anything about it!' will only fuel their anger.

The second and scarier version of anger is inhibited; those who say and show little. Such people will unleash on you without warning ...if you didn't have this book!

Passive aggressive people portray themselves as calm and collected. The passive aggressive people I know will even recite quotes from the Dalai Lama. Don't be fooled; they are suppressing their anger. If you are looking for signs, it is usually to be found in their opinions. For instance, I write a blog on BurmanBooks.com and Facebook.com about how to deal with fear and adversity. I usually get about 10-14 emails with positive feedback for every post. I will also get about 2–3 from people who disagree. Then I will get 1 from someone who is just angry and trying to disguise it under a disagreement. Their anger is clear when I examine the gist of what they write - there is no substance for their reasoning. It's simply an outpouring of negativity and hostility.

Another example is of a person on my team who passes himself off as someone who likes women. Yet when he speaks of women, he uses derogatory terms like bitch or worse. By hearing his words, you can safely assume that he is angered by women in general. Ask a person like this if he is close to his mother. (People who just say yes automatically are usually saying so out of duty and not because they really believe it.) If he says yes, follow-up with how often he sees or talks to his mother. If you make him feel comfortable, you will get a meaningful, lengthy response. A third question to ask is if he has sisters that he is close to. If he does, ask about the relationship, and if not, ask if he has a girlfriend or wife. This will often lead into a discussion about an ex who left him.

If you ask enough questions, you will find the truth. In the case of my team member, his mother was extremely angry after losing two husbands when they left her for other women, so he was sent to be raised by his very angry sister who pushed and beat him during his younger years. He never had a positive female role model - or one who wasn't angry. Instead, he endured a mother who gave him up and a sister who ignored and beat him. He had to curb his own expressions of anger while he was still growing up since he depended on them for his means of living. As an adult, he unleashes his repressed anger on every woman he comes across.

The most difficult part in dealing with passive aggressive people is taking the time to do it. It can take a lot of conversation to get at the heart of the anger they're trying to repress. So take a deep breath. Then, ask the questions and trust that you will find answers that will start to defuse the situation.

6. Fantasy Makers

These people are a lot of work to be around but they are also quite a bit of fun. They have such high in the sky highs and such bottom of the ocean lows. When they are high, they laugh, joke and are excited about life. When they have their lows, Oi vey! They cry, are in despair and experience long depression sessions.

Fantasy Makers are people who build high expectations and when they fall short, they feel completely defeated. I have to confess I am still like that to a certain extent but I watch for it and try to balance it out. I remember getting a green light on a movie at Showtime. It had been packaged by me, which means I represented the author of the book, the screenwriter and was a producer on the movie, all at the age of 26. After about a week of negotiations, the contract was couriered over to me. I had already spent the money in my mind on a new car, new clothes, coke and hookers (just kidding, sort of). The contract arrived the next day and before I could open the envelope, I got a call from Showtime legal affairs department. They told me not to sign the agreement since the movie was dead. Dead? Was there any way I could get a defibrillator and bring it back to life? No, Showtime's budget had been cut in half and because my movie was still in a book form, it would take too long and too much money to develop. I was so depressed, and because I had spent the money in my head, I started to believe I was in debt. This brings on...? Yes, actual debt, since your body lives what your mind thinks.

The reason we create the fantasy in the first place is because we don't equalize the hope with reality. We stay in the warm glow of hope. Hope feels good, since it sends endorphins all over our body. Reality introduces the negative side and urges you to think of a backup plan. Some people are very good at doing this, like my lawyer Bruce. Others need to stay away from any idea of pain due to past experiences and feelings of powerlessness.

These personality types are the easiest to sell to but are constantly in a state of emotional flux, and can end up taking a lot of your energy away with their wild up and down swings.

Taking Down Defences

A human being will always act defensively if you back them into a corner. You will almost always get a reply mixed with some anger. This makes it hard to read a person. However, if you ask your questions gently, the person will show their true colours more often than not.

For instance, if you ask openly, 'Did you steal from my room?' you can try and pick up clues based on micro-gestures and the verbal reply to point to what might have happened. The response might be a short, 'No'. But, if the response is 'No, why is someone stealing? What was stolen?' then you are looking at someone who is telling the truth versus the person who shut the conversation down quickly to avoid being associated with it.

Now, the other way to go about it is by pitching an underhanded ball versus the hardball pitch by stating, 'It's weird, but someone has been stealing from my room.' If the person is innocent, they will most likely ask how you know or what was taken or even offer advice. If they are guilty, it's more probable that they would knowingly place themselves there based on a subconscious reaction and say something like, 'I didn't do it. I would never do that.' Judge by the degree of the reaction - the more vehement, the more feelings - likely guilt - are associated with that reaction.

Sometimes it's smart to go on the offensive and not the defensive. This will provide the groundwork for the potential liar to call themselves out. For instance, if you have contracted a disease, to go and accuse the person you suspect might have given it to you would result in an obvious 'No' or 'Well I never gave it to you, so don't blame me!'. However, if you lay out the groundwork, then simply make a statement, like 'My doctor told me I have somehow contracted mono.' The reaction of an innocent person should resemble, 'I'm sorry to hear! Is it contagious?' The concern for themselves will indicate a fear of contracting it themselves versus a defensive answer due to possible guilt at having given it to you.

Chapter 5

SELF-SABOTAGE

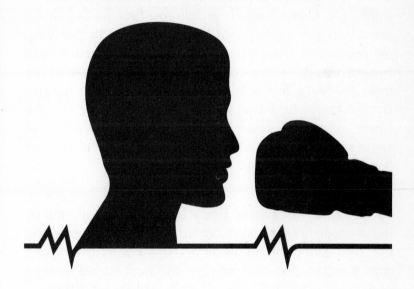

Edmund Bergler, a contemporary of Sigmund Freud, wrote about the 'pleasure-in-displeasure pattern' in his book *The Basic Neurosis, Oral Regression and Psychic Masochism* (1949). It is so important to not only see the signs in of it others, but in yourself too. Sometimes, we actually prefer failure to success and what's more, we'll do what we can to prevent success.

I hated the fact that for so long I was struggling to attain success in my early 20's and yet nothing was coming together as I planned. I wrote in an earlier book, *Do Everything They Tell You Not To Do*, that I went through a period of depression. I was partying all night and sleeping all day because I just wasn't seeing results in my career. The reason came to me after studying this subject. It's called Self-Sabotage, and it happens when the subconscious part of the brain does not believe it is ready or worthy of success. Some people will manifest this syndrome in their relationships and others at work.

To illustrate what your body is doing to you, it's as if the front tires of your car are in drive gear, while the rear tires are in reverse. The car is struggling and wasting gas and energy but isn't going even a centimetre forward until it finally breaks and dies.

I have had the experience of working with some well-known people in my life so far. One of them was a former movie theatre magnate. This man was brilliant. He had a mind so creative he could turn shit into Shinola. The problem was that he developed a physical ailment when he was young which made him an outsider. He was in serious pain all his life from the ailment and was probably bullied. His revenge was to revolutionize the film exhibition/distribution market. His demise? His greed.

After his first failure, he came back on the scene with a bang and formed a live theatre company known for its magnificent set designs and fantastic live shows with major stars on the bill. His demise? His greed.

He was always making good money from his ventures, in fact millions of dollars. He was in the headlines constantly and he was dealing with the top players in Hollywood. Yet, his subconscious still made him feel like he was the abnormal kid who wasn't liked. It pointed out the fact that he would never fit into society and will never truly be liked for who he is and not how much he has or what he could do for people. He was eventually charged and brought to trial for allegedly stealing from his company.

The funny thing about the man is that I really liked him when we went out for lunch. He took me to a deli and we talked about life and his history. I was producing a debate style show for CBC Newsworld and thought he would be a great person to have on the show to debate a very well-known civil rights lawyer. The arrangement seemed to be proceeding well and we talked about it on a number of occasions. However, when we were just about to close, at the last second, he demanded a huge fee, one that surpassed the entire budget of the show.

This man, who'd had his share of very public business controversies, had a great opportunity to show himself in front of the public as a well-spoken and well-educated guy. Instead greed, really the front for his insecurities of not fitting in, took over and he killed his own deal.

I had a company that was bought out by a venture capitalist. The silent partner of the firm was a very wealthy heir to a candy fortune. He put about $5 million into the firm and after I left, I found out he never got a penny back. His partner had moved on to another idea, pulling the plug on the company and refusing to acknowledge that he owed any money. Would you be angry? The heir still talks to the partner and is upset about the money but won't do anything to recover it. Ok, maybe $5 million isn't going to jeopardize his world, but still, to keep in contact with the person that stiffed you? I remember starting my company and needing a measly $200,000 -

this same person laughed at me when I asked him for it. It wasn't the spending of the money that was the problem he told me, it was the fact he wouldn't make much back on a $200,000 investment. So to lose $5 million on a douchebag was more of a risk and 'gambler's rush', but to help a young person get a start in life was not possible.

It's funny because the amount of self-sabotage in that style of thinking is perplexing! However the heir will tell you on his own that he suffers from it every day. He was taught as a kid how to make money. He was told you don't do something unless it makes money. This is why you get multi-millionaires who can't help someone out for a few thousand dollars because it 'won't make money' but will lose millions on frivolous and completely unnecessary expenses like yachts, horses or travelling the world. They do it because in their minds, they are not worthy of what they have. If they inherited it or they happen to make it big from an invention, they don't understand it and they feel guilt from it, so they'll put it at great risk and almost feel a sense of satisfaction when they lose it.

I break the balls (mind the expression) of a media executive who is very powerful and very rich. He

has no kids, no wife and no life. He is totally loyal
to his shareholders, who would replace him in 3
minutes tomorrow if he didn't continue doing his job.
The amount of phone calls he gets would be reduced
from sixty a day to about four. He leaves nothing
behind. All the shows, the stations and the deals will
be forgotten 20 years from now. His life is a constant
turmoil of guilt, sadness, power and image. He could
greenlight a show, put something into development or
put an interview on one of his stations in a heartbeat,
but yet, he doesn't take advantage of any of those
opportunities. It's not because it isn't right or that
favours are never done in Hollywood, but because
he suffers from self-sabotage when it comes to his
personal life. Connecting with another human being
can be a painful experience for him. He chooses to
live his life fully immersed in work to avoid the idea
of pain or betrayal or rejection from an experience
in his past.

A girl I was dating on and off would get very close
to me and then pull back for weeks. Then again,
she would come forward and eventually leave. She
would use the excuse of being busy, but really it was
her way of protecting herself and sabotaging the
relationship. In fact, not long ago, we had dinner and
she told me about a friend of hers who was being led

on by a guy. Her friend really liked him and cried about him all night on the phone with her. Her response to me was, "I would never let a guy do that to me!" From the words she used, you can understand her actions.

My lawyer had a client, an aesthetician who he defended in a civil suit brought forward by a former client who had suffered a hair removal injury. Bruce went against the odds and got the woman off with just a slap on the wrist. She repaid him by writing post-dated cheques and when it came time to cash them, she would call him to tell him not to due to lack of funds. The reason for lack of funds? She was vacationing in Hawaii or Paris. This is the personality of someone where no matter how good you are to them, they will do something to destroy the relationship under the façade of being selfish. They are really scared of having people be good to them, only to let them down in turn.

One last example of self-sabotage involves those people who suffer from a form of masochism. These are people who keep telling themselves and believing that they really want something badly, but still work against it constantly. How many young actors and actresses in Hollywood squander a great start in the movies with unreliable stunts, partying too hard and even criminal behavior?

The problem is that these young people feel the pressure of Hollywood, the paparazzi and the massive fortune they build at a young age. So, the subconscious decides that if they lose the fame, everything will go back to normal. Sadly, many of them end up as just a great story for the tabloids.

Being Too Nice

We love having those people in our lives who will bend over backwards to please us. It's true, even though we may feel a little guilty that they put much more into the relationship than we do into them. What makes them want to overexceed in terms of generosity comes from the insecurity of needing to be liked. My mother is one of those people. If you were to walk into the house and say you liked the sofa, she would give it to you. My father or I would be left with the responsibility of having to haul it out but she doesn't care about that, she only wants the other person to think she is nice and generous. It sucked to have nice toys, because the minute another kid liked it, it was taken from me and given to them. I'm thinking I was abused.

The great thing about having these people around is that they are loyal and almost always happy. Again, it comes down to the idea that they believe if they were to show they were in a bad mood or needed to vent, you wouldn't care or think they were a nuisance and you'd leave them.

The idea of being nice is great. The idea of losing one's self to be liked isn't. A background for people like that is usually feeling like they didn't fit in at school, with the neighbourhood kids or they are very self-conscious. One female friend of mine was almost in tears when I told her she was the 'emotional garbage can' of her friends. I know it sounds harsh, but I wanted her to clearly see how that was and hopefully stop it. She wanted so badly to be liked, she stopped voicing things that bothered her and simply repressed all of them since in her mind she was not important enough for people to take the time and listen. After we had that conversation, one of her friends dated her ex-boyfriend without telling her and she unleashed on her friend with the fury of the Trojan army! I was quite proud of her for finally stating her disappointment in someone else without giving in to the insecurity of whether or not she would be liked after that.

Her insecurity might come from the fact she is exceptionally tall and must have felt awkward in school since most boys are not her height. Feeling like she can be the support system to others might have made her feel that is the way to fit in and get people to ignore how she stands out in a crowd. She is very pretty and has a sincere laugh with a hug that grabs you and holds you tightly; she really needs to understand that her personality alone is all that she needs to fit in. From there, a person can start to create more self-esteem and draw boundaries.

Chapter 6

THE MODEL AND THE TEACHER

It doesn't matter who or what you are going up against, there is a strategy for getting what you want. Anyone who is successful got there by not giving up, by walking into the situation with a pre-determined idea of what they wanted and filling in the gaps with strategy like the ones in this book. This works for any scenario. If you think it through, you will walk in with the advantage, whether it involves business or personal situations.

Intention is everything. Intention walks in the door a quarter of a second before you do. The feeling you process inside is what comes through your eyes. For example, have you ever had a thought about something that made you mad, anxious or sad, and everyone else around you looked at you and asked if you were all right? An internal feeling gets expressed externally before a word is exchanged. If you are walking into a room, think of something cheerful, motivating or funny and you will immediately put your audience at ease.

Mirroring to establish rapport

Creating rapport is creating a connection between you and the other person. The ONLY way to get people to hear you or do as you ask is through rapport. I always like to say out loud when I'm feeling resistance: 'We both have the same goal.' Once, when I was working with an editor over a book manuscript, I could tell she was feeling uncomfortable telling me the uncensored truth. I needed to establish rapport with her to get her defenses lowered. So I said, "We both are trying to make this book the best it can be. So no matter what you tell me, it's to better the book." Once that was said, her comfort level rose and she cut 9,000 words. Ouch.

You can also create rapport through a fondness for sports, kids, jobs, or anything that you have in common with the other person. Rapport can be built within 4 seconds to 1 minute.

NLP or Neuro-Linguistic Programming is a theory and practice for effective communication. Founders Bandler and Grinder created the technique called mirroring. It works like this: if the person you're with leans back in their chair, do the same. If one hand is in their pocket, follow suit. You are establishing a rapport with them. In other words, your energies are getting into sync. Once you do that, you can take control. But, never do it obviously or it will come off as mocking or condescending.

Energy works on a subconscious basis. So, subtlety is essential. It may take only a couple of seconds or an hour for you to lock energy, but once you do, you can test it by shifting yourself and seeing if they follow or looking somewhere else to see if they look with you. Watch what happens when you change your position. Shift your weight and come closer to the table. Lower your voice slightly. Do they do the same? Remember, you don't have to do this exactly the way they do. For instance, if they put their hands up to their hair, you can just put it up to your forehead or face, the effect is still there.

Mirroring is a great technique to use on dates. Sitting in the restaurant, lock eyes with your date. If they are explaining something and make a particular facial expression, follow it. If their hands are crossed in front of them, do the same.

Again, don't mirror obviously! It will come off as a mockery or arrogance. Practice it with friends and family first. If they comment on it, then you have done it too obviously; if they don't, then enjoy the mutual energy you have conjured. Incorporate breathing. You want to be able to breathe in sync with them. You want to maintain the rapport and lead the direction. So if you slow the breathing, if your pupils dilate, so will theirs. If you lower your voice and slow the speech pattern, so will they. When you lean in, they will reciprocate. Once you slow it down, you bring an intimate feeling between the two of you.

Now, this technique can also work in a professional environment. For instance, there was an agent in L.A. who I wanted to work with. My first face to face meeting with the agent was in his office. The moment I entered, I saw a poster for the film *Gladiator*, where he had represented Ridley Scott, the director. I said right away (creating rapport), "Wow, I loved *Gladiator* and have to say Ridley took an action movie premise and gave it so much depth! Congrats, that is a great client to have." He smiled and looked at the poster for a moment which meant he was reflecting quickly on his relationship with Ridley. When we sat down, he looked at his computer to see any emails that had come during the last 2 seconds, so I looked at my phone, which was off anyway, only to create a rapport. Then he sat back in his chair, so I leaned back in mine. Having already looked around his office, I saw pictures of him with many movie stars and noticed he was always fashionably dressed and in great shape. So maintaining eye contact, I commented on how regimented his life was to be so dedicated to his work and being physically fit. I added, "I am going to get into better shape." He leaned forward (taking interest) and told me that he does yoga every morning and maybe I should consider it. I nodded keeping a similar look on my face as he had on his, I answered that I should really look into it (I hate yoga).

Now that I have locked energy, I am in sync and we both are leaning in, I can take control and take the lead. So I looked at the script in my hands and his eyes went to the script. When I looked up at him, he did the same to me. When I reached out to give him the script, at the exact same second, he reached out to receive it. Even with the script in his hands, he didn't look at it, his contact was with my eyes. At the end of the meeting, he had heard every word I said and he wanted to explore how we could work together like we were old friends.

EXERCISE

Subtly mirror someone, family, friend, date or mate. Start with first noticing the small movements and qualities about their body language. Then slowly and subtly start to go into the position they are in. Keep them talking or you talking to keep the attention away from what you are doing. When you do this, make sure you also look interested in what is being said and keep eye contact to make it harder for them to get distracted.

When they switch positions, do the same slowly and within 3 seconds of them doing it. Remember, it doesn't have to be exactly the same, but similar positions. The brain will understand the similarities.

Try to copy their breathing patterns. Hopefully they didn't just come in from a run or you will look like a lunatic.

After about 2 minutes, start to change your position and see if they follow. If they don't, that's okay, go back to the first part and try again. It just means you didn't take enough time to lock energy.

This exercise works like a yawn would, when the one person witnesses it and then starts to yawn themselves.

Chapter 7

PERSUASION

Once you understand the basics of body language and have keen insight into the power of observation, it's not hard to get your way. In a sense, you have to first learn about the person you want something from, then approach them with a knowledge of their own communication style. In other words, I would not approach a man who speaks only French and ask him to become my accountant, until I learned French and was able to communicate with him effectively. Otherwise, wires get crossed. It's the same situation with body language and personality types.

Now persuasion is not mind control. You are not taking away someone's free will. You are simply trying to get them to vote in your favour. If you want chocolate for dessert and your friend wants custard, you will give your friend better results if they agree with chocolate. You are not taking away their free will to say custard at the end of the day, but you are getting them to lean in your direction.

A great way to start persuading anyone to do anything is to present facts from well-known or accomplished people and/or established sources. For instance, when using our chocolate example, you could say, 'A doctor out of Harvard did a study and said that chocolate is actually good for us and reduces the chances of certain diseases.' Now when you have a Harvard doctor saying something, then you are going to get the person's attention. This will weigh heavily when they make a decision. If you know they are addicted to Hollywood gossip, you could include a fact or quote from a famous celebrity.

You have to draw out the whole picture for a person when you are trying to persuade them. You can't just say, 'I like chocolate, and heard it's better for you.' There is no argument, there is no foundation for fact and there is no solution for a problem. Often times we argue like this though. We come at someone from our own perspective and it instantly puts up the other person's defenses since we make them feel insignificant. You're telling the other person, in effect, that your opinion alone counts more than theirs.

Here is a step-by-step approach:

- You must first come to a decision inside yourself as to what you want. You want the chocolate dessert rather than the custard one.

- You then have to come up with why going in the direction they are going in will lead to a negative result. So, custard has egg yolks and sugar, which are both fatty and high in cholesterol. Maybe they have been told that their cholesterol is too high by a doctor already. Maybe they are diabetic. Maybe they don't realize that the heavy dinner with a heavy dessert will end up being too filling.

Either way, you have to get the person to see beyond the wanting of the dessert all the way to the end and what will happen after eating it. This is where the decision is going to start to go your way.

- Then start off with the positives about your choice. The chocolate will be lighter, not as sugary and because it is make with better ingredients, less fattening. You can also add your quote from the doctor or celebrity on the positives of chocolate.

- Finally, tell them how much better it is for them. Make sure you are not dealing with generic ideas but specific details. So an example would be that the chocolate is harder to mess up and therefore there's a higher chance of getting a great dessert as opposed to the lesser possibility of the more complicated custard turning out properly. Or if you are buying it, the chocolate may be lower in cost. The person may have told you in the past that they want to lose weight or change their ways but you're using positive qualities that are hard to dismiss.

Keep in mind, nowhere did I mention anything about stating they are wrong to like custard. This is off putting and will get you into an argument. If it's a passive person, it will shut the conversation down. No one wants to be told that what they like is wrong because what you like is right. You have to convince them of this fact without being rude, insulting or patronizing.

To keep someone engaged, you need to establish rapport. Rapport is simply the connection you make with someone. Remember, a sale is built on emotion, not functionality. We don't buy one car over another because it's better, we buy it because it is safer and thereby better protection for our family, cheaper and therefore we'll still be able to afford University for our child, or blue because it is our favorite colour. So if the salesperson can establish a rapport with you, he will be able to get you emotionally involved with the car.

A great way to build rapport is to allow the person to talk. Don't talk about yourself or your views. People love to talk about themselves, so let them. The more information they give about themselves, the more you will know what you have in common and you'll be gathering details about their story. You can't connect with someone when you know absolutely nothing about them. Remember to use the techniques detailed in the book on reading and reacting to their body language since it will help you see if what they are telling you about themselves is something they actually believe.

Then when you have heard quite a bit about them, speak, but speak little. Talk about the common traits or likes between the two of you. They like baseball? So do you. 'How do you think the Yanks are doing this year?' It will set off a whole new conversation and get them emotionally bonded to you.

Remember mirroring. Use the same voice style. Match their body language without seeming like you are mocking or imitating them. That will further establish your rapport. Once you have connected with them, if you move, they will move. You are looking into their eyes, they are looking into yours.

At that point, start to talk about what it is you want to see happen. Your end result. Make sure you keep them emotionally involved by phrasing it from their perspective and how they would benefit and also demonstrate consideration of their concerns. Once you keep reiterating their concerns and the solution or solutions for them, they will feel much more comfortable with you.

You want to talk in the future tense. Future results gets us out of thinking about present struggles, which includes either the struggle of getting to the future, or the struggle of the decision to buy into you or not. If you talk about the end result, you will get them to imagine a positive result before they even get there!

In today's world, life is about sales. You are constantly selling yourself. To get credit, make friends, get a job, asking for directions, life is about the sell. Without understanding the dynamics of communication, you will lose out on a lot of opportunities that are right at your doorstep.

Keep your vocal tone in mind. I can say something with one facial expression, but my tone of voice and emphasis on certain words can change the entire meaning. Look at powerful speakers like Martin Luther King, Jr., Hitler and John Kennedy - they all understood this rule and if you listen to their speeches, it's the delivery in terms of tone and specific words they hit hard that captivates an audience.

Share yourself. Sometimes when I'm with a resistant person in a situation where I'm asking them to change certain habits in their lives to receive different results, they will become defensive. I will end up sharing something personal about myself at that point that would mirror their current actions and how it was a hindrance to my life until I changed and attained a positive result. You'll see how their body language changes even slightly as they consider it just because you are making the situation relatable.

A great body language reader/persuader is like a Kung Fu master. Nothing is a problem because they roll with every punch and return. So they will read the gestures the person is giving them, predict if it's positive or negative and then estimate the next question or comment about to be launched at them, and no matter what it is, counter with a solution. Remember to listen and watch, because how you should react will be given to you by the other person's behavior.

When you are on a date, making a sale, hiring someone or looking to get hired, ask a lot of questions. Ask, ask and ask more. The more they talk the more you are sending in the following signs to them:

1   You are interested in learning about them
     and who they are.

2. You are thorough.

3. They are flattered because they get to talk about themselves.

Once you are getting all the information out of them, you will also lower resistance between you and them and find common subjects you can expand on to gain rapport. From there, once they are engaged, you can slowly bring them to your side.

Sometimes, your analysis of a situation may make you decide not to pursue a relationship, whether it's business or personal. I had a meeting not too long ago with a woman who had a TV show and she was pitching a book idea. From the first second we sat down at a coffee shop, I felt our energies were 'off'. I couldn't figure out why I wanted to get out of our meeting, but eventually I just started to become more aware of everything she was doing, rather than saying. Her body language had her body sitting erect and stoic. Her elbows were on the table and fingers overlapped over each other, and her facial expressions were almost non-existent. Whenever I was talking about how the process works, she would be looking behind me to see who was coming and going in the coffee shop. She was obviously not listening to me; despite the fact that she was trying to give the appearance of looking smart, she would ask me questions that literally had just been answered. She did that several times and at the end didn't take notes but rather asked me to send her a summary of our meeting. This was obviously because she didn't remember much from our meeting - and we were still having it! It occurred to me that she believed she was a bigger star than she was, but more importantly, her lack of interest in how we work as a company showed me she wasn't interested in a book deal, but rather reinforcing her idea of becoming a star. I could feel a distance and her body language gave me a bit of a cold feeling. I decided to let her know politely that we were the wrong home for her. As far as I know, to this day, she does not have a book deal.

Intimidation scenario: there may be a situation where you are looking to be intimidating. You can follow the rules below in a meeting scenario. We will use a workplace environment and a boardroom as our setting.

1. Always know everything you can about the subject you are going to be discussing and the person you are meeting. For instance, know how much the average

person gets paid, or how much work is involved, or what type of success rate exists. Basic information should be investigated. The person you are meeting, just Google them. It's easy today. There is almost always some kind of information available on them.

2. Get to the meeting a few minutes early and arrange yourself. Have a pen and pad ready.

3. Sit on the opposite side of the table to where the person enters the room. In other words, when they enter the room, they should be closest to the side they will sit on, but have to walk around to greet you. You should always face them as they walk in the room.

4. If possible, sit with your back to the window so they have to face you AND the window. If the sun is shining in and they ask or get up to fix the blinds to avert the sun from their eyes, they are assertive in personality. They will speak their minds and they will butt heads with

you. If they don't and just squint, they are more passive, accommodating and will more likely be non-confrontational.

5. Listen, don't talk as much. Write a lot of notes and make sure it's obvious you are writing a considerable amount of what they say. It shows they are on the record and can be called on it. It also shows they are dealing with someone who is going to be very meticulous. If they are constantly looking at what you are writing, pausing to let you finish writing or circling back on what they say, they are nervous and careful about what they are saying. If they speak confidently, have a great flow and great thought process and look at you even while you write, they are confident and have little to hide.

6. Then ask a lot of questions. Keep your face emotionless, be calm and look them in the eye. You will start to see a lot of gestures occur especially the more quiet you are.

Often times you can just listen to the tone of voice and the choice of words. For instance, if you ask someone 'How is it going?' you might hear a perky 'Fine' or 'Great' or 'Really well'. However sometimes you might get a slight pause or hesitation and a response of 'OK' or 'Good' or even 'It's going'. Almost anyone would know it means that it's not going that well. When you speak to someone and they speak negatively about the future, there is something from the past that is still in their mind that's negative and they have not let go of. For instance if you ask, 'How is your work going?' a response that would show there is something from the past still holding on to them would be 'Ugh, it's tough and there might be lay-offs'. This could mean this person was or came close to being let go at some point in the past and those memories are starting to come back. It's a great technique for getting an understanding of a person's insecurities and thought processes.

If you are not able to discern someone's motivations at first, don't worry because their real intentions will come through if you keep them talking. Just stay cool and observe them. Don't be freakish about it, since the only gesture you will get in return is fear! A person's true intentions will always come through eventually.